Observation, Assessment and P
in Inclusive Autism Education

This practical resource takes a holistic view of the learning and development of children with autism, taking into account the nature of atypical learning and the transactional nature of difficulty. Using an interdisciplinary approach, this accessible and practical text invites practitioners, pupils and parents to reflect on their understandings, beliefs and values and to make appropriate adjustments in their practice. Organised into five chapters, this book covers some of the main issues involved in observation-based teaching and learning, including:

- educational assessment for pupils with special educational needs and disability
- points to consider when observing autistic pupils
- methods for listening within inclusive autism education
- learning outcomes for autistic pupils in relation to well-being, social participation and communication
- compiling pupil profiles that are suitable for autistic pupils.

Aligning research with practice, this sociocultural perspective on autism is of interest to teachers, learning support assistants and SENCos, as well as professionals working in an advisory capacity. *Observation, Assessment and Planning in Inclusive Autism Education* will also be of interest to students on courses that cover autism as well as anyone who wants to develop their practice and find new ways of supporting children and young people.

Carmel Conn is a Senior Lecturer in Special Educational Needs at the University of South Wales, UK.

Observation, Assessment and Planning in Inclusive Autism Education

Supporting learning and development

Carmel Conn

LONDON AND NEW YORK

First published 2016
by Routledge
2 Park Square, Milton Park, Abingdon, Oxon OX14 4RN

and by Routledge
711 Third Avenue, New York, NY 10017

Routledge is an imprint of the Taylor & Francis Group, an informa business

British Library Cataloguing in Publication Data
A catalogue record for this book is available from the British Library

Library of Congress Cataloging-in-Publication Data
Names: Conn, Carmel, author.
Title: Observation, assessment and planning in inclusive autism education :
    supporting learning and development / Carmel Conn.
Description: New York, NY : Routledge, 2016. | Includes bibliographical
    references and index.
Identifiers: LCCN 2015035190 | ISBN 9781138842069 (hardback : alk. paper) |
    ISBN 9781138842106 (pbk. : alk. paper) | ISBN 9781315731827 (ebook)
Subjects: LCSH: Autistic children—Education.
Classification: LCC LC4717.5 .C65 2016 | DDC 371.94—dc23
LC record available at http://lccn.loc.gov/2015035190

ISBN: 978-1-138-84206-9 (hbk)
ISBN: 978-1-138-84210-6 (pbk)
ISBN: 978-1-315-73182-7 (ebk)

Typeset in Sabon
by Apex CoVantage, LLC
Printed in Great Britain by Ashford Colour Press Ltd

MIX
Paper from
responsible sources
FSC
www.fsc.org   FSC® C011748

Contents

Figures

Tables

Preface

The two books in this series, *Observation, Assessment and Planning in Inclusive Autism Education: Supporting Learning and Development* and *Play and Friendship in Inclusive Autism Education: Supporting Learning and Development*, have the aim of presenting an educationally relevant and inclusive approach to supporting autistic pupils in schools. At present, the field of autism education is dominated by specialist practices that are strongly influenced by a medical model of individual difference and deficit. Many of these are hard to implement in ordinary classrooms and serve to exclude autistic pupils from the outset. These books seek to provide an alternative approach to educating pupils with autism, one that promotes observation-based pedagogy, partnership working and respect for difference and diversity. Reflection on children's learning and everyday experiences at school – practitioners sharing their reflections with others, including parents and pupils – is at the heart of these processes and is seen to be what underpins best practice in autism education.

Children's learning and development are located within social contexts and involve social processes that are transactional in nature. Within both these books, a sociocultural perspective on pupil learning is taken, which views the child or young person within an environment that includes other people's communication, understandings and ways of interacting. Inclusive autism education is described as an interactive process of teaching and learning that is embedded within social relationships and involves situated learning. The view put forward is that education should be less concerned with individual psychology and more with developing rich contexts for learning that support the participation of all pupils.

Importantly, a sociocultural perspective is concerned with patterns of behaviour and what is shared within communities of practice, but also with seeing the value in difference and diversity. Locating learning and development within the sociocultural environment requires withholding judgements about what pupils know and can do until a proper understanding of pupils' experiences and ways of making sense of situations is gained. This involves taking steps to gain information about pupils' perspectives and giving them a voice within the teaching and learning process. It also involves practitioners, pupils and parents reflecting on the understandings, beliefs and values they bring to contexts of learning, and making appropriate adjustments following these reflections. A sociocultural perspective on autism is of interest to the progressive practitioner who wants to develop their practice and find new ways of supporting children and young people.

Up-to-date research findings and relevant theoretical ideas are presented in both books in accessible and practical ways. Since autism education is concerned with what is most fundamental in human development – that is, communication and social sharing – an interdisciplinary approach is used. Understandings from developmental psychology are discussed within parts of the text, but these are presented alongside ideas taken from other disciplines, including childhood studies and disability studies. An educational perspective is interwoven throughout as a way of aligning research with practice, ensuring that ways of working and forms of support are always oriented towards ordinary teaching and learning processes. It should be noted that an interdisciplinary approach provides practitioners and parents with a greater understanding of children's social worlds and enables them to see what is different in the behaviour of autistic pupils, but also ways in which these pupils are the same. It enables them to see what belongs to the individual, but also what is part of group processes, what are the pupil's social difficulties and learning needs, but also what are the pupil's strengths and important interests.

The intention here is to highlight what theory means to ordinary practice in schools, but the emphasis is on the central importance of practical knowledge in autism education. Practical knowledge is the everyday understandings that practitioners hold about the pupils with whom they work, and the knowledge about their child that parents contribute too. Ways of working and forms of learning support promoted in these books are 'bottom-up' in the sense that they centrally use people's practical knowledge – that is, knowledge of *specific* interactions and relationships, features of *particular* learning environments and *unique* personal experiences. Inclusive autism education is more concerned with children's actual social experiences, interactions and relationships – and less with generalized ideas about what these might or should be – and this fact makes practical knowledge the starting point in teaching and learning.

The ways in which we choose to describe phenomena is critically important to how we understand it. A strongly medicalized discourse dominates autism theory and practice at present. This uses a normative discourse and describes autistic children in terms of their 'deficits'. A further aim of the two books in this series is to help to insert another form of words into discussions about autistic children, their play, interactions and friendships, and their education, learning and development. To this end, terminology use is carefully considered throughout. Person-first language (i.e. child with autism) and the terms 'autistic child' and 'autistic pupil' are both used here. This is used respectfully to reflect current professional language use, but also the preference of some people in the autistic community who see person-first language and its use only where a characteristic is viewed negatively, as contributing to the construction of negative identities (Sinclair, 2009).

Chapter 1

Taking an educational perspective on the autistic pupil

Focus of this chapter:

- current understandings about the autism spectrum
- good practice in relation to autism education and the central importance of assessment to teaching and learning
- two models of disability, the medical model of disability and the social model of disability, and their implications for education
- educational assessment for pupils with special educational needs and disability, with special reference to autistic pupils.

Introduction

UK and European guidance on the education of pupils with special educational needs and disability recommends that ordinary methods of assessment are applied within inclusive education (EADSNE, 2009; Wilkinson and Twist, 2010). These methods, which include observation, listening to children and teacher reflection, are suited to gaining an insight into how children and young people make sense of the world and participate in learning. They enable school practitioners to reflect too on their own knowledge, understanding and practice as a way of providing effective support for learning. Knowledge, understanding and reflection are key aspects of autism education, and the aim of this book is to outline a reflective approach to observation, assessment and planning that is useable within inclusive autism education.

At present, theory and practice in relation to the education of pupils with autism take a strongly medicalized approach. This focuses on the individual child and their impairment and promotes a skills development model of learning. This book describes an alternative approach to autism education based in observation-based pedagogy that provides a better 'fit' with ordinary educational practice and makes more sense given the socially contextualized nature of social-emotional learning and development. A holistic and naturalistic perspective on children's learning is offered, and clear guidance is provided on how to view the autistic child within everyday contexts that are rich, interactive and involve other children's and adult's interests, understandings and responses. Ordinary methods in observation, listening to children and adults, recording and reflecting on information, and identifying next steps in learning are outlined, together with explanations of the adjustments and special considerations that need to be made in the case of autism.

Autism education is concerned with children's early capacities in communication and social sharing that are the basis of human development. It has a strong focus on children's social-emotional learning and on their experiences of interactions, roles and relationships. It could be argued that autism education is most aligned with practice found in the early years and in reflective teaching, which also takes an interest in children's interactional and communicative experiences and the ways in which they make sense of these. Early years practice and reflective teaching promote observation-based pedagogy as a way of seeing the whole child within ordinary contexts, and listening to children as a way of gaining insight into their perspectives. These methods help us to understand how children's actions relate to their understandings and patterns of thought, and know how to provide support for learning appropriately, naturalistically and at the child's level. Observation, assessment and reflective practice are very ordinary aspects of teaching and learning, yet are mostly neglected in the literature on autism education. This book explores the rich possibilities these methods offer in terms of enabling educational practitioners to gain knowledge and understanding and so support the learning and development of pupils with autism.

Current understandings about the autism spectrum

There can be no doubt that our understanding of autism has changed significantly in the last few decades. Not only has there been a remarkable rise in the number of reported cases of autism, but also there have been important changes in what we know about autism and how it affects people's lives.

Prevalence rates

Perhaps the most dramatic development in our understanding of autism is the rapid rise in diagnosed cases. Autism was once thought of as a rare disorder, but this can no longer be said to be the case. Prevalence has increased steeply, from 1 in 5,000 of the population being on the autism spectrum in the 1970s to 1 per 1,000 in the 1980s, and more than 1 per 100 of the population in 2009 (Baron-Cohen et al., 2009). The most recent estimate in the US provided by the Centers for Disease Control (CDC) puts the figure at 1 out of every 68 children, or 14.7 cases per 1,000 of the population (CDC, 2015).

The increase in people being diagnosed with autism is partly explained by the wider use of the diagnosis, the earlier age of diagnosis and inclusion of milder cases, but the cause of autism is still not fully understood. We know that autism has a genetic base, but there are also thought to be risk factors involved, such as parental age and diabetes in pregnancy. It is probable that the numbers of cases will continue to rise, though current figures are largely gained from Western high-income countries with little evidence currently about prevalence around the world.

Diagnostic criteria

The fifth revision of the American Psychiatric Association's *Diagnostic and Statistical Manual of Mental Disorders* (APA, 2013), known as DSM-V, has rationalized our understanding of the autism spectrum by proposing that the separate diagnoses of autistic disorder, Asperger's syndrome, childhood disintegrative disorder, PDD-NOS and Rett syndrome should come under one diagnostic category: autism spectrum disorder. Figure 1.1 illustrates the new definition of autism spectrum disorder put forward in DSM-V. This recognizes the highly integrated nature of 'social interaction', 'communication' and 'imaginative play', and describes the difficulties associated with autism as being within a single domain of functioning, that of social communication. DSM-V proposes that autism is more simply defined as difficulties in social communication together with the existence of stereotyped or repetitive behaviours and interests, which includes sensory behaviours.

Autism is now understood to be a subset of an 'autism phenotype' which describes people who may not be diagnosed with the condition, but who nevertheless have autistic traits, such as poor eye contact or poor awareness of other people's feelings. The 'autism spectrum', therefore, should be thought of as a dimensional difference and on a continuum with the general population.

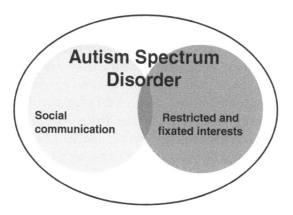

Figure 1.1 New definition of the autism spectrum proposed in *Diagnostic and Statistical Manual of Mental Disorders*, 5th edition (DSM-V) (APA, 2013)

Relationship to gender

Autism is something that is known to occur in boys more than girls, but it is becoming increasingly apparent that more girls are affected than was previously thought. Most recent estimates suggest that autism is likely to occur about four times more often in boys compared to girls (Newschaffer et al., 2007). However, the incidence of autism in girls is far from clear since it is apparent that there are different factors operating where girls are concerned (Nichols et al., 2009). Girls with autism appear to be better at masking the condition. They display more behaviours that appear to be social – for example, copying other peers in a group – and have special interests that are more socially oriented – for example, an interest in people's hair or the sensory details of clothing. It is the case too that different social expectations exist in relation to girls. The expectation that girls are quieter than boys, for example, has an impact on a process of diagnosis that is based on one person identifying characteristic behaviours in another. A girl who is socially withdrawn may be more likely to be perceived as depressed rather than having social communication difficulty, whilst associated eating difficulties in autism may result in a girl being diagnosed as having an eating disorder.

Population variation

Wider use of the diagnosis has also underpinned a shift in our understanding about how autism manifests itself in people's lives. We understand now that, though autism is characterized by differences in social interaction, verbal and non-verbal communication, sensory processing, and by restricted interests and behaviour, there is significant variability in how these differences are experienced by people with autism. Research into the experiences of play, interaction and friendship for children and young people with autism necessitates a rethink of the classic image of the autistic child: of a child in a world of their own, who does not seek out interaction, does not play and has no friends. Research evidence shows children and young people with autism are at least partly socially engaged, though differences exist in the form their engagement takes compared to children without autism. Autistic children do play, though they have particular play preferences, they tend to have at least one friend, though that friend may have also have some sort of additional need, and it is likely that development in social communication will occur, though this may require more in the way of support than is the case for other children (Bauminger and Shulman, 2003; Chamberlain et al., 2007; Jarrold and Conn, 2011). There is great variation in all these areas of functioning, with some individuals existing outside of any kind of social relations, whilst others are centrally involved within social networks and cultural contexts.

Educational provision for pupils with autism

The wider use of the diagnosis of autism has meant a change in the profile of an autistic person. More people who might once have been described as having 'mild autism' are being diagnosed, and there is less association now with learning disabilities, though this remains a feature of autism for many people. This together with the introduction of the inclusion agenda in special education has meant a rise in the number of pupils with autism being educated fully or partly in mainstream classrooms. In the UK, it is estimated that around two-thirds of autistic pupils are currently included within mainstream schools (DfE, 2014).

Educational provision for children and young people with autism is more widely understood to require an 'eclectic approach' that involves a range of practices and support mechanisms (Kasari and Smith, 2013). Autistic pupils are conceived of as being able to participate and learn to some degree within ordinary contexts that are suitably adapted. However, they are also seen as needing to learn to compensate for development that does not take place in ordinary ways and that requires aspects of specialized provision.

Good practice in autism education

In the UK, the Autism Education Trust (AET) has developed a set of standards for the delivery of best practice in educational provision for autistic pupils. These are based on research carried out into existing good practice in schools identified through school inspection as centres of 'outstanding' or 'good to outstanding' practice. The report, *What Is Good Practice in Autism Education?* (AET, 2011), identifies eight themes as markers of quality in the education of pupils with autism:

1   *high levels of ambition and aspiration* for autistic pupils, with a priority given to enabling them to reach their potential both academically at school and in future adult life;
2   the establishment of *effective systems for monitoring and recording learning progress*. Schools should use a range of bespoke learning outcomes, taken from the National Curriculum as well as other adapted social-emotional curricula, within an approach that also evaluates the usefulness of learning support strategies. The ways in which information about a child's learning progress is recorded and shared amongst practitioners and parents are a further important feature of practice. Recording methods should include written records but also, importantly, visual recording methods, such as photographs and video;
3   a *combined approach to the delivery of the curriculum*, using adapted forms of the National Curriculum alongside autism-specific programmes that target goals in social communication and behaviour. Schools should emphasize

developing individualized learning packages to meet pupil's individual learning profiles that include adapted lessons, differentiated learning tasks and adjustment of expectations about learning outcomes;

4   *joint working across children's services* within multi-professional teams that include health and education professionals, especially for the purpose of identifying children's learning needs, developing individual learning plans and designing programmes of support. Close working and regular liaison meetings with a range of professionals should be seen by schools as an important form of support for children's emotional health and well-being, for daily living issues and family support, and for the development of children's social communication;

5   *well-trained and dedicated staff* who use a 'quality-first' approach to teaching that supports everyday inclusive practice and personalized learning for pupils. Strong and supportive leadership is important as is clear vision about aims and purpose of autism education. Schools should emphasize training as a key aspect of practice, including training of staff as well as staff with expertise and knowledge about autism disseminating good practice;

6   the establishment of *effective communication systems* for staff and between staff and parents as well as effective listening to children. In schools, practitioners should dedicate large amounts of time to communicating with each other about pupils' progress and make themselves readily available to children and parents. A variety of communication forms should be used, including observation of others' practice, regular staff meetings, student councils and surveys, and written, phone, email and face-to-face contact with parents;

7   *involvement in the local community* for the purpose of supporting understanding and acceptance of autism. Schools may see themselves as 'autism ambassadors' with a role in raising awareness within the wider community. Good practice in specialist settings involves making strong links for joint activities and integrated experiences with local mainstream schools;

8   the establishment of *strong relationships with children and families*. Schools should see the building of understanding relationships as a starting point for supporting pupils' learning and well-being. Partnerships with parents should also be prioritized as a way of sharing knowledge and understanding of pupils, carrying out joint planning of educational practice and delivering consistency across communication. Support for families at home should also be seen as an important area of working.

Importance of assessment for learning

What Is Good Practice in Autism Education? puts an emphasis on the use of 'quality-first teaching' in the education of pupils with autism. Quality-first teaching is an idea introduced in UK government guidelines on effective inclusive practice in schools (DCSF, 2008b) and makes reference to the fact that quality in ordinary teaching practice is the key to success with all learners. High-quality teaching involves teachers having clear objectives for lessons, which they share with pupils, using a lively and engaging teaching style and maintaining high expectations of all learners, as well as providing support for the language content of lessons and maximizing the use of visual, kinaesthetic and other forms of learning.

An important aspect of quality-first teaching is that the teacher responds to the ways in which learners individually engage with their learning to create 'personalized learning' contexts that maximize pupil engagement and progress. The day-to-day interactions between teacher and pupil in the classroom are seen as the basis for the effective development of personalized learning, teachers taking time to gain knowledge about the attainment of pupils and the progress they are making. Teachers should gain knowledge of each pupil's learning from active and continuous assessment and build strong relationships. They should continuously prompt pupils to demonstrate what they know and can do within supportive and encouraging environments, and should also reflect on their own practice as well as the experience of learning for individual pupils.

This qualitative type of assessment is known as formative assessment or assessment for learning. It differs from summative assessment – assessment *of* learning – that is used to measure pupils' attainments at the end of the delivery of curricula. Assessment *for* learning is generally carried out by class teachers and other professionals as part of everyday practice and involves the following:

- gathering information by making observations and asking questions;
- recording information in a variety of ways;
- reflecting on information with pupils and adults;
- making assessments of learning and progress.

What is learning?

Children's learning is an emergent process that is integrally connected to the context in which it occurs. Learning is not context-free, but is situated and involves the child participating in 'communities of practice' – including sociocultural routines, cultural ideas, texts, signs and symbols – in increasingly complex ways (Wenger, 2009). Children's agency and ways in which they make sense of and participate in lessons are crucial to the process of learning. It is the case that learning is located *within the learner* and how they make sense of learning experience, and not within the imparting of instruction by the teacher, though this may be an important source of guidance and support (Black and Wiliam, 2003).

Assessment for learning is useful for teachers and other practitioners because it informs them about pupils' learning experiences and guides them to the next steps in planning. It celebrates diversity and values all pupils' achievements, but is not overly concerned with measurement of attainment and does not hold children accountable for what they know. The emergent nature of learning means that pupils are in the process of acquiring knowledge which is not always testable in more formal situations. Assessment for learning has attracted a good deal of interest in recent years since it is thought to be the most effective way of adding value in terms of children's attainment (Wiliam and Leahy, 2007).

Assessment for learning and special educational needs

Assessment for learning is considered just as relevant to the education of pupils with additional learning needs, though forms of assessment may need to be adapted or adjusted. Practitioners may be required to spend more time observing children, for example, or work harder to interpret pupils' contributions and reflect on their own practice. However, assessment for learning impacts upon the educational chances of all pupils and often determines whether a child or young person experiences exclusion or inclusion. The personalized learning agenda is viewed centrally within effective inclusive education practice and is seen as the key to success in moving all pupils forward in their learning and development.

How can we view the autistic pupil for the purpose of assessment for learning?

Assessment for learning involves the construction of a rich picture of the pupil and the ways in which they think and behave, looking particularly at how they make sense of and participate in learning contexts. The process of assessment is envisaged as one of revealing a pupil's existing knowledge, conceptual understandings and how they see the world. The purpose of doing this is to enable the teacher to make pedagogical decisions about how to engage pupils at the right level to further their learning and move them on in terms of understanding.

Gaining insight into how pupils make sense of and participate in learning contexts is not a straightforward exercise, but must be viewed as particularly problematic in the case of pupils with autism. Autism involves a subjective experience of the world that is highly individual and different to that of non-autistic people. It is a subjectivity that is based on sensory-perceptual experiences – that is, what the person sees, feels and can remember – much more than on social understandings that are brought to perceptions of the world. Someone who does not have the condition and sees the world in socially mediated ways does not easily understand the subjectivity of an autistic person. Milton (2012) describes this as the 'double empathy problem', where both parties – autistic and neurotypical – experience difficulty in understanding the point of view of the other. People with autism are described as lacking a theory of mind, but it could be argued that people without autism also lack a theory of the 'autistic mind' and how it perceives the world in non-social ways.

Given the issue of differential subjectivity in autism, how then can we view the autistic pupil for the purpose of assessment for learning? Two important models for describing disability and children's learning needs – the medical model and the social model of disability – have been applied to autism and are described next.

Medical model of disability

The medical model of disability has dominated the way in which we view the autistic child or young person, both in education and for the purposes of research. This is a model that views disability as a result of individual impairment or lack of skill and so 'belonging' to the individual. Figure 1.2 illustrates the focus of the medical model of disability, which is the individual, their biology and individual psychology. The medical model of disability arises from research that identified stages of 'normal development' and focuses on what the disabled person cannot do in relation to these, measuring their 'deficits' against 'standardized norms'.

View of the child

The view of the child within the medical model of disability is one of 'typically developing', where development is viewed as a natural progression through individual stages of growth towards an endpoint of being 'fully developed' (Woodhead and Faulkner, 2008). Children are conceived of as being on a developmental pathway that is the same for all children, though some may progress along it at a slower rate and in a limited way. Developmental stages are universal, applicable across populations and largely unrelated to social and cultural influences. According to the model, the disabled child is viewed as 'disordered' or 'abnormal', the child conceived of as deficient in some way when measured against 'normal development'.

Implications for education and learning

The normative measures that are a key feature of the medical model of disability are used to delineate what needs to be supported in terms of children's learning and development. Precision in identifying very small steps within stages of growth is seen to be important as a way of being able to identify and measure what is happening for a child in terms of development, particularly one with a disability. The idea of 'remediation of skills' is a central one since this addresses the fact that disabled children must be taught certain skills to overcome aspects of their impairment and so be helped to progress within 'deficit areas' of development. The focus is fully on the individual child and ways to facilitate their development in discrete areas of functioning – for example, in mental capacity, language, attention, understanding and so on. Drill and practice teaching techniques are emphasized over

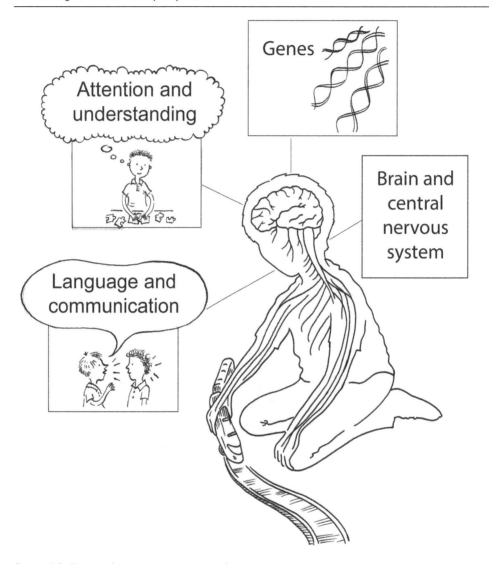

Figure 1.2 Focus of the medical model of disability

exploratory learning, and development itself is conceived of as the product of growth in discrete cognitive areas, which can measured against statistical norms if they are adequately described as single areas of functioning.

Key terminology

Individual behaviour, stages of development, deficit, intervention, skills, norms, measurement.

Social model of disability

The social model of disability is associated with the rights-based agenda of the disability movement and was devised as a response to the medical model of disability. The social model of disability puts forward the idea that a person's disability can be located within their experience of social relations and the ways in which difference and diversity are accommodated and thought about within society (Thomas, 2013). The distinction is made between 'disability', which is seen as socially constructed, and 'impairment', which describes simply what the person is bodily not able to do (Burke, 2012). The focus of the social model of disability is much less on the person with impairment and more on the attitudes, values and systems they encounter as well as cultural practices, institutions, policies and norms. Social change is seen as the way forward, with the idea that disability may be much reduced, or even not exist, given certain social structures.

View of the child

The social model of disability is aligned with ideas in childhood studies that see the child as a socially functioning individual, a 'social actor' who makes sense of, participates in and contributes to social practices and norms. The idea of stages of development is accepted, but with much greater emphasis on the agency of children in helping to create the worlds in which they participate and learn. The child's environment, which includes immediate social relations in their families and communities as well as influences that exist within the wider social world, is seen as critical to the way in which development unfolds, determining the quality of the child's experience, the ways in which they engage and so the nature of their learning. Figure 1.3 depicts the focus of the social model of disability and illustrates the fact that all children exist within sociocultural worlds that are made up of other people, their language, understandings, expectations, practices, interests and concerns. The multiple and diverse influences that exist within children's lives underpin the fact that they should be not thought of as a homogeneous group but defined in terms of their difference and diversity. Disability is viewed as a form of diversity that should be seen, therefore, in terms of childhoods that are already diverse.

Implications for education and learning

The social model of disability takes a wide view of learning and development. It locates disability and any learning need not straightforwardly within the learner but in the structures and relationships with which they engage. Support for learning involves environmental adjustments and adaptations, including other people's behaviour, expectations, values and understandings. Children are envisaged as being able to participate more fully in their learning if they are adequately supported by their teachers and parents, and in this way to progress and develop. The

Language and communication of all individuals within the setting

Understandings and expectations of adults

Personal interests, shared practices, skills and perspectives of other children

Organization of the play space and materials available

Figure 1.3 Focus of the social model of disability

social model of disability is interested in children's competencies and interests, seeing these as the basis for their learning and development.

Key terminology

Shared impairment, attitudes and understandings, strengths, sameness versus difference, diversity, social contexts, social processes.

Two perspectives: Micro-level and macro-level

The medical and social models of disability imply different points of view, but it could be argued that the experience of disability is not an either-or situation. Essentially, the medical model provides a close-up and extremely detailed perspective on the individual, a 'micro-level' view that can provide interpersonal, intrapersonal and even neurological information. The social model of disability provides a wider view that is focused on the person *plus* their environment and the wider socioculture. It is a 'macro-level' view that is not able to give detailed information about one person, but is able to give extremely important information about the world of which they are part, the expectations they encounter and the quality of their experiences.

Across children's services there is a need for a balanced view that is able to take in both biological and sociological features of children's lives (Watson, 2012). At times a micro view is required – for example, for the purpose of medical investigation – but at other times a macro view is needed – for example, within education as a way of thinking about and developing learning contexts and reducing barriers to participation. What is important is flexibility of view so that the most useful perspective on children's lives is used at the appropriate time, and so that one view does not obscure other important areas of investigation.

Each model – medical and social – involves its own discourse, or ways of describing, and it is vitally important to take this into consideration. Use of language determines how phenomena are seen and understood, and adjustments in language can open up new ways of thinking about, engaging with and supporting children's learning and development. Examples of discourse that are relevant to our thinking about autistic children would be as follows:

Medical model of disability (micro-level)		Social model of disability (macro-level)
individual child	–	dyad / group
impairment	–	social process
disorder	–	strengths
behaviour	–	context
truth	–	personal perspectives
universality	–	difference and diversity
individual skill	–	participation of all
single variables	–	integrated variables / holistic
science-based enquiry	–	local enquiry
intervention	–	reflective practice and learning supports

The capability approach to special educational needs and disability

Within disability studies, it has been suggested that the difficulties inherent in taking a perspective on diversity can be overcome by the capability approach. This is a framework developed by Sen (1992) to describe poverty and equality, which has also been seen as of relevance to special educational needs and disability. The capability approach focuses on the person and their ability to realize the type of life that they want to lead. Rather than seeing disability as the result of physical impairment or social structures and norms that affect people in the same ways, it views disability as irreducible to the idea of a common condition and as always located within the way the individual experiences personal, external and circumstantial factors (Terzi, 2005). Disability is related to a person's particular characteristics, including their individual impairment, but also to features within their physical, social, cultural, economic and political environment. The ways in which these different variables interrelate with each other are different for different people and determine the nature and extent of individual disability, including whether disability is actually experienced.

The capability approach puts forward the idea that disability must be assessed not as an objective evaluation that applies across a population but *in a subjective way*. Disability relates to how a person is more or less able to convert the resources they have available to them to meet their own objectives and values. In outlining the capability approach, Sen is less concerned with people's actions or behaviours and more with their interests. Disability is the result of someone not being able to become or to do what they value in terms of 'being and doing'. Sen frames the situation as one of a person having a 'capability set' that consists of their own personal resources plus their external opportunities and supports, which together allow them to achieve desirable 'functionings'. Functionings may be activities that a person wants to do – for example, to communicate, to play or to have a friend – but also involve desirable states of being – for example, to be understood, to feel in control and to be free of stress. Individual disability is assessed on the degree of divergence between what a person values in terms of being and doing and what they are actually able to succeed in being and doing, with the idea that both sides of this equation may change over time (Bellanca et al., 2011). Competencies, rather than what someone cannot do, are a focus, but only alongside a consideration of the existence of enabling factors within a person's environment.

The application of the capability approach to autistic people is problematic since it assumes there are intrinsic values that are shared across individuals – for example, to be well-nourished, to be safe, to flourish and so on. It is arguable in the case of autism that some values viewed as 'basic' – for example, to be social – are experienced intrinsically. Nevertheless, the idea of disability being viewed pluralistically, subjectively and as the result of an individual-ized set of internal and external factors is eminently useful in thinking about autism. Autism is characterized by the degree of variation in well-being, health, impairment and disability across the population, with the way in which per-sonal resources and external factors within a person's capability set intersect and interrelate playing a critical part in this. Autism is known as a 'transac-tional disability' (Jordan, 2005), and two autistic pupils who have a similar level of impairment may have completely different experiences of disability as a result of differences in the communication, understandings and attitudes they encounter within their respective school settings, with difference experienced not only in their social environments but also within their physical and sensory environments.

 Reflective task

List five features of practice in autism education that you think are key to children's learning and development. Prioritize them from most to least important, thinking about your reasons.

Find a partner whose list differs from your own. Compare your priorities and explore any differences of opinion that exist between you. How are your priorities a reflection of your experience, understandings and values? Think about:

- your beliefs about the nature of disability in autism
- your understandings about learning and development in autism
- the purpose of inclusive education.

Medical versus educational assessment

The medical model of disability has dominated autism research and practice for over three decades and uses a micro view of the autistic child. This sees devel-opment as individually based and describes very small stages within 'develop-mental norms' that are each identified as a discrete area of functioning. Within autism practice, such descriptors are frequently promoted as the method best suited to assessing autistic pupils and measuring their progress following an intervention or teaching programme. Table 1.1 provides an example of this type of medicalized approach – in this instance, to the assessment of play. Different aspects of play that are thought to be relevant to development are listed and the pupil's achievements recorded according to these, perhaps following a series of observations or conversations with practitioners and parents. There are no qualitative descriptions of play, and other forms of children's play are not included. Such an approach may seek to reflect what is happening within group processes too – in the example here, in peer play – but the focus of assessment remains the individual behaviour of the child with autism, and not the behaviours of others in their peer group, the activity being carried out, the play materials that are being used or the responses of adults who are overseeing the play.

This kind of assessment reflects medical diagnostic assessment, which may include some qualitative descriptions of the contexts of behaviour, but is more

Table 1.1 Assessment of children's play based on developmental 'norms'

1. ASSESSMENT OF PLAY
Cognitive levels

	L	O	S	N
Sensorimotor play – plays with properties of object	✓			
Functional play – plays with toys according to their function		✓		
Relational play – combines objects in meaningful ways				✓
Pretend play				
– imagines properties and uses of object			✓	✓
– invests emotion in play				✓
– provides a narrative to play actions				✓
– takes on a role in play				

L = Learned; O = Occasional; S = Supported; N = Never

2. ASSESSMENT OF PEER PLAY
Behaviour

	L	O	S	N
Observer role				
– interested in peers and watches what they do		✓	✓	
– stands on edge of peer groups				

	L	O	S	N
Parallel play				
– sits near		✓	✓	✓
– shares play materials				
– copies others' actions				
Shared play				
– follows peers' instructions			✓	✓
– shares play goals				✓
– takes on different roles				

L = Learned; O = Occasional; S = Supported; N = Never

likely to focus on very small units of individual behaviour. Autism as a condition cannot be seen directly and is at present identified as a set of characteristic behaviours. Diagnostic assessment in the case of autism is for the purpose of identifying personal difficulty that is measured against these. Applying a medicalized micro-level approach to assessment within inclusive autism education, however, raises a number of difficult questions. Diagnostic assessment of autism focuses on behaviours such as poor eye contact, 'flatness' of emotional expression, body posture and gesture, participation in social interaction and sensory processing differences. By contrast, educational practice is not necessarily concerned with teaching these same behaviours. For example, though a pupil with autism may be found to have poor eye contact following diagnostic assessment, it is not educationally useful or indeed ethical to teach them to make eye contact. Once a child is diagnosed as having autism, education is much more about achieving a balance between support for pupil learning and development – which may be viewed as atypical in nature – and acceptance of their disability, difference and diversity.

Purpose of educational assessment

Educational assessment has a different purpose to medical assessment. It is concerned with the individual pupil, but in respect of the learning contexts in which they engage. The aim of education is achievement in learning, and the ways in which pupils participate in contexts for learning determine degrees of success in this. Autistic pupils are engaged in adapted learning contexts, and the formative assessment processes that are so critical to success in everyday teaching practice should be seen as of relevance to them. Formative assessment – assessment for learning – has little use for normative measures. Descriptions of small units of behaviour provide large of amounts of information about the individual pupil, but give little indication of how to support their 'development-in-context' (Webster et al., 2004) – that is, what adjustments need to be made and supports provided within the pupil's actual learning environment. How the child or young person compares to an identified 'typical population' is of little use to the practitioner who is trying to support friendship *with this other child* or inclusion *in this play context*, where all children's capabilities, efforts and concerns are of interest.

Narrow descriptors of behaviour have the added problem of highlighting some aspects of behaviour whilst overlooking others. Again taking play as an example, descriptors often focus on children's participation in forms of play that are thought to be cognitively important whilst overlooking other types of play viewed as less so, even though these might be ones with which autistic children are more likely to engage. Overlaying typical behaviour onto the behaviour of the child with autism increases the likelihood of not seeing the atypical development that is probably occurring. It is likely that autistic children experience, understand, act, communicate and develop in differential ways that are missed when neurotypical measures are applied. A medicalized approach to educational assessment thus contributes to rigid thinking about pupils and their development and a non-acceptance of difference and diversity. It may also contribute to parental anxiety that their child is 'not developing' or 'insufficiently developing'.

The purpose of educational assessment will be one or all of the following:

- to support and scaffold pupil learning;
- to plan teaching and the delivery of curricula;
- to evaluate the effectiveness of teaching and learning.

Educational assessment is part of the process of teaching and learning and involves practitioners reflecting on what pupils know and can do in order to be able to think about and plan next steps in learning. It enables the provision of effective learning support, which in turn can be evaluated and any new learning reflected on once more. Educational assessment happens over time, the process of assessment being a cyclical one of looking, reflecting on, planning and reviewing. There is no clear educational endpoint of 'being developed', and learning is seen more as a lifelong endeavour.

Educational assessment for special educational needs and disability

Educational assessment for pupils with special educational needs and disability (SEND) would have the same purpose as for all learners. The process of assessment would also be the same, though there may need to be extra consideration of certain areas of functioning. Given children's particular needs – for example, in communication – it may be the case that assessment of pupils with SEND is carried out in slightly different ways, with more intensity, for a longer period of time and with the use of supports.

Assessment and learning for pupils with SEND involve the following key considerations.

A holistic approach

Children's learning and development are holistic and should be assessed in relation to areas of functioning that are viewed as highly integrated. Generally speaking, children develop in all parts of their life more or less equally, with developing capacities in one domain contributing to development in other domains. Holistic assessment views the pupil as a whole person who grows in physical, intellectual, social, emotional and moral ways that are intricately bound up together. Children's learning takes place not just in school but in all aspects of their lives, and within experiences that contribute to development in ways that can be foreseen but that are also unexpected. Assessment methods must be sufficiently powerful, therefore, to take account of learning that has been planned for, but equally for learning that has not been planned and that takes place in relation to different settings.

This integrated view of learning and assessment should also be applied to pupils with SEND, who may experience difficulty in one or more areas of functioning but who nevertheless learn and develop in ways that would be described as holistic. It is a model that is particularly helpful in thinking about autism because it most accurately describes early learning and development. Autism education is concerned with the early learning experiences in communication and social sharing that support later development, and these must be thought of as highly integrated in terms of the cognitive, social-emotional and psychomotor components.

Consideration of the child's ecology

Children's learning and development relate to the contexts in which they occur. It is 'situated learning' that cannot be viewed as separate from the influences and processes present within the environment of which the child is part – that is, the child's ecology. Children interact with their environment and participate in learning experiences, moving themselves forward in terms of their understandings and capacities with the support and encouragement of those around them.

Children's immediate environment, which includes familiar others, is the most important learning context, but this in turn is shaped by wider social influences and processes. Bronfenbrenner (1979) described an ecological systems model of development where different systems – ranging from the immediate and local to wider social systems, cultural practices and norms – are in continuous interaction and help to shape each other. Though the child may not be in direct contact with wider societal systems, nevertheless these serve to influence those who are in contact with the child and the institutions and communities of which they are part.

Ecological assessment refers to the assessment of a child's functioning within differing contexts. It views the child's behaviour as related to features that are present within specific settings with the idea that the child may function differently in different environments and within different relationships. The fact of this, moreover, is not seen as a case of simple cause and effect but as probably the result of a number of interrelated influences. For example, at school, it is the case that a pupil may be settled and attentive within a small group that takes place in a quiet space facilitated by a certain member of staff, but become much more anxious within different groups and larger and busier environments where different personnel are present. Ecological assessment views the pupil's experiences of relationships as key to their learning and these relationships themselves as the result of multiple and diverse influences. An adult who is supporting a pupil may bring ideas and values about children's learning and participation based on their own historical experiences of childhood, membership of cultural groups and societal values. These ideas will partly determine the nature of relationships in the here and now and provide an important influence on learning outcomes.

Consideration of the ecological aspects of learning is particularly important for pupils with SEND. The inclusion agenda frames pupils' learning needs as partly the result of features within their learning environment – for example, the knowledge, understanding and attitudes of school practitioners, and the nature of roles and relationships within pedagogy (Florian, 2008). It is attention to the healthiness of the child or young person's ecology that reveals whether their differential participation in learning contexts can be more effectively accommodated and learning progress made.

Practitioner knowledge and understanding are seen as the key issue of autism education (Jones et al., 2009). Autism challenges our understanding of an experience of the world that is differential, partly non-social and highly individual. Features in the environment influence the behaviour of the autistic pupil, but these may not be readily apparent or easy to understand. The 'double empathy' issue of autism creates challenges to ecological assessment, but the barriers to learning that invariably exist for pupils with autism make it nevertheless vitally important to do such assessment.

Recognition of children's agency

An important aspect of the assessment of pupils' learning is the idea that children are engaged *actively* in learning contexts. They are not passive recipients of learning, but are continually trying to make sense of learning experiences as they participate in them. The ways in which pupils cooperate in their learning, how they understand tasks and interactions within tasks, and the way in which they utilize learning tools will all be reflected in their learning outcomes. Pupils with SEND are also active and intentional as learners, also making sense of experience and contributing to the development of their understanding and construction of knowledge. This is the case for pupils with autism too, though, again, it might be more difficult for educational practitioners to ascertain how an autistic pupil is making sense of things. The differential and partly non-social subjectivity of autism means that the child's perspective and ways of making meaning are not easily apprehended and may never be fully understood by practitioners. However, recognition of the agency of the autistic pupil is just as important in understanding their participation in learning contexts and knowing how to support them and move them on in terms of their understanding.

'Tuning in' to the child

The idea of an adult 'tuning in' to a child is related to the concept of attunement in early child-caregiver relationships. Attunement refers to the ways in which adults work hard to receive young children's communications and attempts at social sharing, not limiting their attention to vocalizations and verbal forms of communication only, but showing an interest in all aspects of communication. In attunement, the adult is highly sensitive to the child's non-verbal forms of communication, to the child's attention, social orientation and the emotional quality of the relationship. Non-verbal communication is a particularly important feature of children's communication, children communicating more than adults through their behaviour, sounds, gestures, movement, rhythm and also in their silences. Adult attunement is a creative and intuitive 'listening with all the senses', therefore, that is capable of receiving children's communications in whatever form.

Non-verbal communication is an important part of older children's communication too, and can be a particularly important feature of the communication of pupils with SEND. The concept of 'tuning in' remains relevant to all pedagogical relationships and to the assessment of what pupils know and can do. Within special educational needs, the concept of 'fine-tuning' (Dickins, 2008) refers to the fact that some pupils require the adult to work harder at tuning into their communication, which may be indirect and unclear. This is especially the case for pupils with autism, whose social communication can often be delayed, weak and easily missed by those around them, though much better understood by those who know them well.

Use of ordinary methods

Educational principles for pupils with SEND are not fundamentally different to those for all pupils, though the process and intensity of teaching and learning methods used may be slightly different. From an investigation into the use of assessment for learning procedure with pupils with SEND, the European Agency for Development in Special Educational Needs (EADSNE) found that ordinary assessment for learning approaches are just as relevant to the assessment and learning of pupils with SEND:

> All children have needs, some children have special needs. What is good for SEN is good work for all pupils. The better the quality of education the more pupils with SEN can be included.
>
> (EADSNE, 2009: 5)

However, EADSNE envisaged the task of the educational practitioner as one of adapting assessment procedure and considered that some methods are especially important. Amongst these are the use of observation as a way of tuning into the particular nature of learning for pupils with SEND, the use of flexible modes of communication that are tailored to the needs of the child or young person, and the compiling of individual portfolios that facilitate the sharing of pupils' learning experiences by practitioners, pupils and parents.

As with all children with communication difficulty, observation has particular importance for the assessment of pupils with autism since it provides the practitioner with the most access to the autistic pupil's particular experience of the world, ways of understanding and forms of communication. Making observations of pupils in informed and systematic ways is a well-used method in educational assessment, particularly in the early years, and involves the practitioner reflecting on their own understanding and knowledge of the pupil and their own practice in relation to pupil learning. This process of reflection takes on even greater importance for the practitioner who is making assessments of autistic pupils because of the differential subjective experience of the world that is operating. More thought and analysis of what has been observed will probably need to be a part of day-to-day assessments, as well as the practitioner comparing their understandings of the pupil with other adults' and with other sources of information about their learning.

Listening to children is another method typically used in educational assessment that uses questioning of children and a focus on their talk in natural settings. This is also applicable to the assessment of pupils with SEND, including pupils with autism, but again may need special consideration. Attention will need to be paid to the level of language used in talking to pupils, to how questions are framed and to the use of support for communication, such as visual support systems, but it is the case that listening to children with SEND can yield important and unique information about their learning experiences.

Use of a shared network

In addition to the use of a range of methods, educational assessment for pupils with SEND should involve the use of checks within methods to ensure reliability of the evidence about learning progress (Frederickson and Cline, 2009). The use of different sources of information is helpful since it allows a process of 'triangulation' or verification of information that has been gathered. The use of a shared network, which includes practitioners, parents and pupils, provides a further check within methods. Rather than a single practitioner making assessments of the pupil and analysing and interpreting information by themselves, assessment should be viewed as more of a collaborative exercise, where professionals compare findings and discuss possible interpretations. Parents should be seen as part of this shared network, their unique understanding and knowledge of the child seen as a vitally important source of information, particularly in the case of autism. Children and young people who are able to review information about their learning can also form part of this network, their contributions and that of their peers often providing further clarification about an experience that has been observed.

The process of educational assessment for pupils with autism

More will be said in the next chapters about the use of ordinary methods of assessment, with descriptions provided of the particular adjustments that can be made when assessing autistic pupils. Figure 1.4 shows the cycle of assessment for learning in inclusive autism education. This illustrates that assessment of pupils with autism does not differ from ordinary assessment for learning, though it does emphasize shared reflection, careful focusing on specific issues and consideration of both strengths and difficulties within contexts.

Educational assessment for learning of autistic pupils critically involves the following key processes.

Looking

Observation of pupils' activity, participation and responses is the starting point for making assessments of their learning experience and progress. Different methods of observing can be used, including formal as well as informal ones, but assessment of the autistic pupil at this stage concerns seeing them within context, taking a wide view of their engagement and gaining detailed knowledge and understanding of their environment, which includes the personal resources, interests, understandings and responses of other people, both children and adults. Of interest are patterns of engagement and disengagement, competencies as well as difficulties, and the transactional quality of experience.

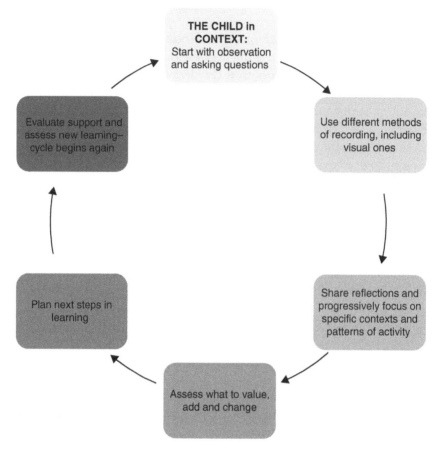

Figure 1.4 Cycle of assessment for learning within autism education (adapted from DCSF, 2008a)

Listening

Listening and asking questions of children and adults, including parents, support observation. Listening is for the purpose of clarification or for gaining more detailed information about an issue. Framing questions, particularly those addressed to children and young people, will require attention to language use and probably involve simplification of language and the use of visual information. Some autistic pupils may not be responsive to questioning, but some will and asking pupils questions is an extremely important way of giving them a voice within the assessment process.

Recording

Recording assessment information can involve different methods, including written descriptions, diary entries, taking photographs, gathering examples of children's work and using questionnaires and observation schedules. Visualizing children's learning experiences – that is, creating pictures and other visual representations – is important since this provides a useful tool for sharing information with pupils about their learning, gathering their perspectives and supporting further learning through reflection. All forms of documentation of pupil learning contribute to the assessment of learning progress and the creation of a 'picture of development', which can be stored as evidence of attainment within pupil portfolios.

Progressive focusing

Assessment for learning in autism education is far from straightforward. It requires understanding the autistic pupil's differential ways of making sense of the world and experience of learning contexts, but it also involves making judgements about contexts for learning and the degree to which they support pupil learning or put up barriers. Enquiry, moreover, needs to be made into the appropriateness of the pupil's participation within *particular* settings and relationships. The transactional basis of disablement for autistic children means that predetermined categories of developmental 'norms' and generalized ideas about social roles and practices will be of less practical use than local practitioner knowledge gained from everyday interactions. An overview is needed of the cultural norms, social understandings and practices that operate in a setting, and the competencies and difficulties of individual children assessed in relation to these.

Shared thinking

It is important to review assessment information within a collaborative process that involves educational practitioners, parents, children and the multi-professional team. The 'double empathy' issue in autism means that extra effort and shared thinking are necessary as a way of avoiding mistaken assumptions and wrong conclusions. Review can take place informally, in conversations between practitioners, between practitioners and pupils, between practitioners and parents, and within the multi-professional team. It can also be carried out within more formal meetings, which have the purpose of identifying learning targets or planning provision.

Each of these processes in assessment for learning will be described in more detail in the chapters that follow. These look in turn at methods in observing pupils, ways of giving pupils a voice and gaining their perspectives within the process of assessment, and how to identify pupils' attainments, learning needs and appropriate learning supports. Throughout the book, key points for practitioners to consider are described as a way of developing reflective practice and the effectiveness of these support strategies.

Chapter 2

Making observations

Focus of this chapter:

- observation as a method of educational assessment
- points of consideration in relation to observing autistic pupils
- the purpose of observation in inclusive autism education
- lines of observational enquiry in relation to autistic pupils
- specific methods of observation, including participant observation, event sampling, ecological observation, mapping and time sampling.

Introduction: Observation as a method of educational assessment

Looking at and noticing the world around are a constant part of our experience and something most of us take for granted. Observing children and young people within education, however, involves looking with more of a clear purpose and noticing in a more organized way. When we observe pupils we watch them as they go about ordinary activities and also listen to what they say. This is in order to gain knowledge and understanding about their experience and how they are making sense of the world so that we are able to engage with them as learners. Educational practitioners, particularly those who work in the early years, are familiar with the educational purpose of observation, but educators in the later years sometimes feel that watching children is doing nothing. They often think they need to act in some way, to intervene, to make a comment on children's activity or 'to teach'. Yet observation within education is a key feature of teaching practice and can provide a powerful form of support for pupil learning.

Observation is about tuning in to children and young people and learning about what they can do. It is about seeing the whole child within ordinary learning contexts and gaining insight into development that is context-based. Observation is an educational approach that is suited to the complexities of social learning and the interactive, dynamic and emergent nature of children's development. Learning takes place within the learner and is contingent upon the pupil's experience of and participation in learning contexts. It is not something that is 'done to' children, as it is often envisaged within autism theory and practice. In her book on child observation, Fawcett describes educational observation in the following way:

> Observation is about taking children seriously, hearing what they have to say, respecting their interpretations, and valuing their imagination and ideas, their unexpected theories, their exploration of feelings and viewpoints. We can learn about children through watching and listening in an alert and informed way that raises awareness and sharpens understanding.
>
> (Fawcett, 2009: 15)

Observation provides information about children's patterns of behaviour, their skills and abilities, their learning styles and achievements, their levels of development, and also their learning needs. Importantly, it allows a pupil's strengths as well as their gaps in learning to be identified. Observation across settings provides information on pupil participation in different contexts, where different influences, norms and practices operate. This can be extremely useful for the autistic pupil, who may not be as flexible as other children and not as able to adapt to different environments. Seeing the whole child within natural contexts enables us to make assessments of development within component areas – social, physical, intellectual, communicative, emotional – that are highly integrated and need to be considered together. Crucially, observing autistic pupils within ordinary educational contexts provides a strong link between theory and practice – that is, linking an understanding of autism and how it manifests in people's lives with the individual pupil with autism and their actual learning experience and developmental needs within particular settings.

Points to consider in relation to observing autistic pupils

Observation is the starting point in the cycle of educational assessment, but we should not assume that what we see when we observe children interacting and communicating is what everyone sees. When we look at and listen to others within a setting we bring our subjective self to the experience, using our understandings, ideas, values, personal history, beliefs and opinions to interpret what it is we are looking at and listening to. These aspects of ourselves can determine what it is we even notice and what we do not see or dismiss as not relevant. Our subjectivity is not something that we can 'get over', but we do need to be aware that it exists and we need to reflect on what we have brought to the act of observing when thinking about our findings.

Becoming an effective observer within education is about developing the following skills:

- being precise about the purpose of an observation;
- preparing adequately before making an observation;
- keeping an open mind about pupils' activity and not allowing preconceptions to influence your interpretations;
- committing to developing understanding about an issue gained through depth of thought and the suspension of judgement;
- having self-awareness and reflecting on personal understandings and beliefs;
- analysing findings adequately, probably in collaboration with others, following an observation.

Extra care and consideration are required when carrying out observations and analysing information gathered about a pupil with autism. In particular, the following features of autism as a condition should make us cautious about interpreting children's behaviour and coming to conclusions that are too hasty.

 Think! *Autism involves a differential subjectivity*

Having autism means processing experience in highly individual and partly or mostly non-social ways. It involves a different kind of consciousness that does not automatically apply social meanings and understandings, but focuses more on the sensory and perceptual qualities of experience, which might hold little or no social meaning. People with autism describe a differential subjectivity that is varied in the way the sensory aspects of the condition are experienced and strongly individualistic in the way that meaning is created. Autism involves a 'private language' (Williams, 1996) that is idiosyncratic in nature and cannot easily be shared.

Observation and the process of assessment in education focus on pupils' perceptions and ways of making meaning, with the understanding that personal experience, if carefully investigated and reflected on, will yield meaning that the practitioner can know and understand. There is the notion of a shared framework of communication that can be richly tapped by the conscientious and reflective teacher. The differential subjectivity of autism, however, means that a shared framework of communication is reduced and may not be available in the case of some autistic pupils, particularly those in more specialist settings. It is the 'double empathy problem' (Milton, 2012), described in Chapter 1, where non-autistic people lack an understanding of the 'autistic mind' and how it perceives the world in non-social ways. The educational practitioner will have to work harder at interpreting the autistic pupil's activity and needs to share their interpretations with others. They may also have to accept that they will never fully know and understand a child, and of necessity operate with a continuing sense of uncertainty about their own practice. This makes monitoring and the ongoing cycle of assessment an extremely important feature of practice within autism education.

🐛 Think! *Autism is an invisible disability*

Invisible disabilities are disabilities that cause impairment and real challenges for the individual, but that are difficult for other people to see and acknowledge. Problems in recognizing a disability because of a lack of visible evidence can mean people do not fully understand the cause of someone's difficulty, and this in turn can lead to expressions of doubt that difficulty even exists.

Autism is sometimes described as an invisible disability. Many people with autism have no obvious physical signs of impairment, though there might be small, subtle signs that are evident to someone who has an awareness of the condition. It is also the case that more able autistic people might actively take steps to reduce outer signs of difference and mask signs of difficulty.

Invisibility also refers to the fact that the behaviour of the autistic child may be experienced as challenging by others without the influences on that behaviour being clearly seen. Children may be stressed because of social communication demands, sensory processing difficulties and their need for predictability. Small triggers may eventually lead to major upsets because of a build-up of stress, but none of these things might be obvious to the people around. Figure 2.1 illustrates the hidden nature of autism, which was depicted by Schopler (1994) as an iceberg with only part of the condition visible as specific behaviours, but the greater part invisible though forming the base influences of those observed behaviours. Stress builds when we are under mental or emotional pressure and affects how we feel, think and behave. It can affect us at a body level that might be outside of ordinary awareness, but nevertheless results in a hormonal release and 'fight, flight or freeze' response which precludes being

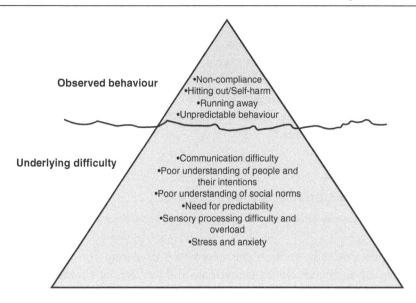

Figure 2.1 The iceberg analogy for autism as an invisible disability (adapted from Schopler, 1994)

able to think about and control one's behaviour. But stress is not something that is clearly visible, and sometimes we are not aware ourselves how stressed we are.

 Think! *Autism involves atypical development*

Though autistic children do tend to develop in terms of their awareness, understanding, sociability, language, communication and intellectual capacities, it is not clear that they follow a 'typical' developmental pathway. It seems more likely that autistic children develop in some ways that are the same as other children, but also in ways that are fundamentally different. It is possible that autistic people learn to compensate for some aspects of development, becoming more consciously aware of social behaviours and developing learned social strategies that non-autistic people carry out much more automatically (Kasari et al., 2001). It also appears to be the case that autistic people, particularly those who are high-functioning, develop social interaction styles, forms of communication and patterns of friendship that differ in varying degrees from those found in the neurotypical population (see e.g. Bauminger et al., 2008).

The atypical development of autism means that when we observe and make assessments of autistic pupils we need to bear in mind we are not looking at development as one might expect to see it. Observing children is partly concerned with thinking about and making comparisons with ordinary expectations in child development, but it is important within autism education to consider that 'expected development' may operate differently and that typical development is not the only standard to use.

 ### Think! *The emotional impact of autism*

Research indicates that, though the experience of caring for any child with a disability involves greater challenge, parents and teachers of autistic children, particularly those who present hard-to-manage behaviour, experience even higher levels of stress (Lecavalier et al., 2006). Parents experience greater physical demands, social demands and also financial demands. They also encounter negative attitudes and lack of understanding from the general public, which can be an important source of anxiety and depression. Teachers of autistic children also report higher levels of tension, particularly where they feel that communication with and instruction of a pupil are not manageable in ordinary pedagogical terms (Emam and Farrell, 2009).

When working with autistic pupils, some of whom struggle considerably within educational settings, practitioners might experience strong emotions that give rise to the idea they need to act quickly and decisively (Billington, 2006). Nevertheless, taking time to observe, think and reflect on children's experiences is as important for autistic pupils as it is for all pupils and can be the quickest way to providing effective support for their well-being, participation, learning and development. Awareness of what we bring emotionally to an observation is something upon which we also need to reflect. If we are experiencing difficulty in managing a child's behaviour, a sense of hopelessness about our abilities as a practitioner and criticism by others of our practice, or alternatively, if we are experiencing positive experiences of communication with a pupil and appreciation of our work by work colleagues, this will strongly influence how we look and what we see when we observe.

The need for reflective practice

Taken together, these features of autism mean that practitioners must proceed with extra caution when observing and assessing an autistic pupil. We know that in autism education a shared framework for communication and understanding does not operate in the same way as it does for typically developing children. There is greater need for reflective practice, depth of thought and the sharing of ideas and interpretations, and for these to be ongoing features of practice. We need to pay attention to how we describe the pupil and their activity, trying to avoid making judgements and acting on intuitions that may be wrong (Powell and Jordan, 1993).

 Reflective task

Read the following observational account of the playtime experience of an autistic pupil. Identify in what ways it is subjective and what assumptions are being made by the practitioner who has recorded it. Discuss the key elements of a more objective observational record.

> In the playground, Leroy went over to a girl and aggressively snatched the ball she was holding, making her protest loudly. He kicked the ball angrily into a no-go area of the playground, looking round to the midday supervisor to see if she was going to tell him off. When she made no comment, Leroy fetched his ball and then kicked it again into the area, trying to push boundaries. After some time, Leroy went to a small group of peers who were playing on the swings. His support worker told him to stand near her and help push another boy who was on one of the swings. Leroy did this, but then sat on a swing himself and asked to be pushed. The boy who had been swinging eagerly jumped down and started to push Leroy, but he found it hard to coordinate his pushing of Leroy's swing, which moved erratically and with little force. Leroy started to get angry with the boy, shouting, 'You're not playing with me!' and pushing the boy forcefully away with his swing. Eventually, the support worker had to intervene. Leroy was left to himself and pushed his swing, trying to jump on it whilst it was in motion. He tried to do this several times, but it was hard to get a satisfactory swing in this way and he eventually gave up.

Autism as cultural difference

In thinking about being objective, it is useful to consider a perspective on autism that views having the condition not as pathology but as cultural difference. This view emphasizes the fact that autistic people share an experience of individualistic perceptions and private meaning making and an interest in sameness, and that this gives rise to distinctive ways of thinking, patterns of behaviour and cultural norms (Straus, 2013). Autistic people could be described as making sense of the world in novel ways that are fundamentally different to non-autistic people, but that are shared across the autism population. Accordingly, people with autism are not 'stuck' developmentally, but develop atypically with different learning profiles that produce different, but shared, patterns of behaviour:

> In a sense, autism can be thought of as a culture, in that it yields characteristic and predictable patterns of thinking and behavior in individuals with this condition. The role of the teacher or parent of an individual with autism is like that of a cross-cultural interpreter: someone who understands both cultures and is able to translate the expectations and rules of the non-autistic environment to the person with autism so that he or she can function more easily and successfully. To work effectively with individuals with autism, we must understand their culture and the strengths and deficits that are associated with it.
>
> (Mesibov et al., 2004: 19)

The notion of cultural difference and cultural interpretation is also relevant and is linked to ideas about cultural misunderstandings and 'culture shock' (Davidson and Henderson, 2010). The process of viewing practices, norms and ways of being that exist outside of our experience and understanding often gives rise to feelings of unfamiliarity, strangeness and perhaps even criticism and negativity. Understanding autism may mean having to overcome difficult feelings and involve a struggle to grasp something that feels beyond us. Educational practitioners and parents may have to work hard to develop an understanding of the experience of autism and constantly need to reflect on the differences between the subjectivity of the child they know and their own.

Viewing autism as cultural difference also means that 'misunderstanding' and 'interactional difficulty' should be reflected on in terms of the whole setting and not seen in relation to the autistic pupil only. Autism is a transactional disability, where difficulty can be experienced on both sides: by the autistic person but also by the individual with whom they are interacting. Within pedagogy, it is very important to consider how this 'shared impairment' is viewed and described for the purpose of observation and assessment.

The purpose of observation in inclusive autism education

Observation is part of professional practice in education and an important method for learning about children and knowing how to support their development. Pupils' learning relates to the contexts in which they engage and to the ways in which they participate in practices with other people. Autistic pupils also participate in social contexts, though their participation may be less and much more individualistic. The purpose of making observations of autistic pupils is the same as for all pupils, though with some special considerations. Specifically, we observe autistic pupils in order to:

- 'see' them more clearly and tune in to their communication;
- look for strengths and what to build on;
- notice what they move towards and their positive emotional responses as a way of understanding their engagement in learning;
- notice what they move away from and any negative emotional responses as a way of understanding stress factors within the environment;
- look for patterns in social participation and identify learning needs;
- note the responses of peers;
- share our observations and thoughts with others and reflect together on our knowledge, understandings and practice;
- ensure that planning is based on pupils' actual experiences of learning;
- carry out regular observations as a way of achieving ongoing understanding of the pupil's engagement in learning contexts;
- monitor the development of new capacities in the pupil over time and assess progress in learning;
- align autism education with ordinary educational practice.

Observation is systematic looking

In order to achieve quality in terms of observational practice, it is important to look and listen in systematic ways, ones that are planned and properly organized. Frameworks for observation are helpful since these provide a structure for looking and listening. A simple frame to use for observation involves being specific about:

- *who* is being observed, whether the individual autistic pupil, the autistic pupil and their peers, a peer, or other groups of children and adults;
- *what* you want to find out about – in other words, what is the focus of the observation;
- *where* the observation takes place and any connection between location and observed activity;
- *when* the observation takes place and in relation to what activity or event. It is often useful to compare observations that are carried out in different contexts and at different times of the day or days of the week;

- *how* you are going to carry out the observation and the reasons why the method you choose is suited to the aim of the observation.

Good observations are made when practitioners focus on what the pupil actually says and does, and try to be specific about what they record. Practitioners should document what they observe concisely and in an organized manner that is as objective as possible. Observations should be carried out regularly within a process of continuous assessment, and practitioners should seek to compare and contrast their findings with those of other people.

Informal and formal observation methods

Methods of observation differ and provide different kinds of information about children's experiences. An observation might be informal, such as spontaneously noticing that a pupil does something whilst you are engaged with them, or it might be more formal in that you have planned to look at an issue as you interact with children, or it might be highly formal and involve careful planning and structured looking 'from the outside' at what a pupil or group of pupils is doing. A range of methods is described in this chapter, some of which are informal but can have formal elements introduced, and others that are strictly formal. Which method you choose depends on what you want to investigate, but key features of formal and informal methods are as follows:

Informal For example, participant observation		Formal For example, time sampling
Observer is engaged or partly engaged with what is being observed	–	Observer is outside of what is being observed
Incidental or pre-planned	–	Planning is always required
Records information within a narrative account	–	Records information within a schedule or structure
Probably takes a wide, ecological view	–	Probably takes a narrow, individual-based view
Should be a starting point for assessment for learning	–	Provides focused investigation of an issue that has been highlighted by another method

Important lines of enquiry in relation to autistic pupils

In formulating questions about children's learning and development, it is helpful to follow certain lines of enquiry. As with all learners, enquiry into the autistic pupil's progress in relation to literacy, numeracy and other aspects of the common curriculum will be important. In addition to this, four further areas of competency that are particularly relevant to pupils with autism in inclusive education are offered here:

1 The child's or young person's *emotional well-being*, ability to cope with stress and self-regulate in the school setting;
2 The child's or young person's capacities in relation to social and cultural *participation*;
3 The child's or young person's capacities in relation to non-verbal and verbal *communication*;
4 The child's or young person's capacities in relation to *making sense of the world*, particularly in relation to the attribution of social meanings within their learning.

These areas of competency are designed to address the atypical learning and participation of children with autism, but they are not a definitive list or a prescriptive set of developmental levels, though they are developmentally informed. What are provided are indicators to significant areas for investigation in autism education. Some areas of functioning and inclusion will not be appropriate for some autistic pupils, whilst other areas not highlighted may need to be a focus. Lines of enquiry are designed to support *but not dictate* professional practice, with practitioners, parents and the multi-professional team viewed as best placed to make decisions about the actual process of observation, assessment, planning and evaluation in their setting.

Reflection is on social contexts more than individual behaviour

Children's learning and development cannot be viewed as separate from their social context. Following lines of enquiry about the autistic child and framing questions for reflection about contexts for learning involve investigating strengths and difficulties of the individual child *in consideration of* environmental conditions, influences and supports. Only in this way can assessment for learning be truly useful and fair. Reflection is on the child in relation to their experiences of communication, roles and relationships, much more than on individual behaviour linked to predetermined categories that define what a 'normal child' should be doing at a particular age. Innovation in early years curricula, such as New Zealand's influential early childhood curriculum, Te Whāriki (New Zealand Ministry of Education, 1996), provides a way forward in trying to locate children's learning within its context. Early years curricula ask questions about the child, but equally and at the same time, about the sociocultural environment.

Reflection is on children's cultural routines

In autism theory and practice, 'what is social' has been largely defined as people's immediate interactions with each other. Sociocultural theory, however, tells us that 'what is social' must also be thought of in terms of the knowledge we have of the wider sociocultural world and our facility in using cultural materials and practices. Ochs et al. (2004) argue persuasively that we must work towards 'an enriched view of autism', one that conceptualises what is social as interpersonal engagement as well as sociocultural knowledge and understanding. In making observations of children as they interact and play, it is important to investigate what cultural routines exist for these particular children in your setting. Children's cultural routines are the activities, interests and practices with which they engage on an everyday basis and which are informed by children's interpretations of the sociocultural world around. Routines differ for different children and across settings, but remain fairly stable for individual children and peer groups over time, children engaging in the same play themes and maintaining the same cultural interests often over years (Corsaro and Johannesen, 2007).

In making observations of the social participation of the autistic pupil, it is vitally important to know what cultural routines exist for them and around them, and the quality of social communication in the setting generally. What social competencies do other pupils have and how is communication experienced by them (e.g. do other children use a high proportion of non-verbal compared to verbal communication)? What do children talk about and what games do they play? What aspects of the wider culture do children appropriate in their play and interactions *in this setting* and how are they interpreted and used? How do adults support them in this and what cultural knowledge do they bring? Teasing out the fine details of children's everyday interactions to answer questions such as these is critical to a holistic assessment of social competencies within the group and, in turn, the appropriateness *within context* of the participation of the individual pupil.

Lines of observational enquiry are presented here separately, but the approach to observation and assessment should take an integrated view of children's activity, learning and development. Children's emotional responses, their capacity to participate, interact and communicate, and their capacity to create social meanings in relation to learning experiences are all intricately linked and are not a set of separate skills. Seeing these different areas of enquiry as parts of a whole is therefore important, as is cross-referencing between areas of investigation. Lines of enquiry are linked to the learning outcomes that are provided in Chapter 4.

EMOTIONAL WELL-BEING

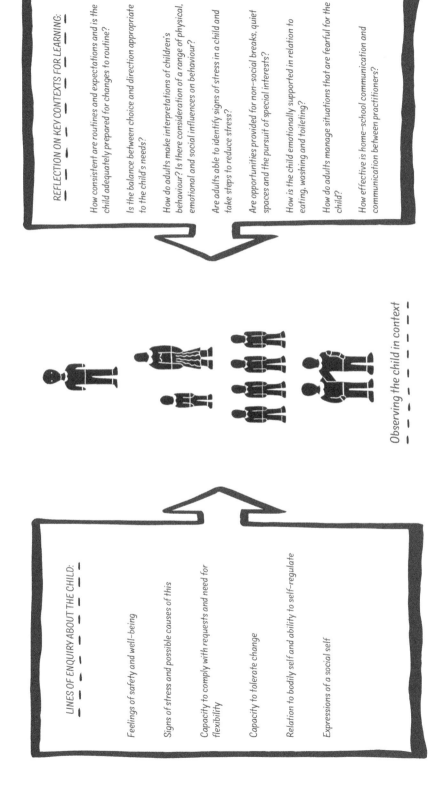

REFLECTION ON KEY CONTEXTS FOR LEARNING:

How consistent are routines and expectations and is the child adequately prepared for changes to routine?

Is the balance between choice and direction appropriate to the child's needs?

How do adults make interpretations of children's behaviour? Is there consideration of a range of physical, emotional and social influences on behaviour?

Are adults able to identify signs of stress in a child and take steps to reduce stress?

Are opportunities provided for non-social breaks, quiet spaces and the pursuit of special interests?

How is the child emotionally supported in relation to eating, washing and toileting?

How do adults manage situations that are fearful for the child?

How effective is home-school communication and communication between practitioners?

LINES OF ENQUIRY ABOUT THE CHILD:

Feelings of safety and well-being

Signs of stress and possible causes of this

Capacity to comply with requests and need for flexibility

Capacity to tolerate change

Relation to bodily self and ability to self-regulate

Expressions of a social self

Observing the child in context

PARTICIPATION

What patterns of activity in play and interaction exist? Are these visualized and explained?

What cultural resources do all children draw on in their play and interactions?

How are play opportunities and the play space organized?

How much enjoyment do children derive from their play?

What social roles are children adopting in play and interaction? How often do these lead to conflict?

How do children describe themselves and each other and when does criticism occur? How is conflict thought about and managed by adults and children?

How are all children's interests, strengths and ways of doing things valued and accommodated within the setting?

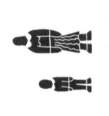

Observing the child in context

LINES OF ENQUIRY ABOUT THE CHILD:

Strengths in participation in play and interaction routines with adults and children

Comparative facility in producing culture within the setting

Shareable nature of special interests and ways of doing things

Changes in participation over time

Perceptions of the child's participation by children and adults

Responses to challenge within social experience and need for experiences of non-participation

COMMUNICATION

REFLECTION ON KEY CONTEXTS FOR LEARNING:

In what ways do adults simplify language and support it with visual information?

Is sufficient time for responses given by adults and children?

How do children make sense of each other's communication? What is the 'fit' in communication of individual children? Are children's communication forms appropriate to play and interaction routines?

What is the quality of children's talk and what do they talk about? How is media culture used?

What misunderstandings occur within communication and how are they resolved? Who notices difference in communication and what do they do?

Is there consistency of communication between practitioners and between home and school?

Observing the child in context

LINES OF ENQUIRY ABOUT THE CHILD:

Details of uses of communication, looking at non-verbal and verbal communication, and including visual communication

Relationship of non-verbal to verbal communication

Purposes of communication

Contexts in which communication and attention to communication are at an optimum

Importance of ICT to the child

Feelings linked to communication

MAKING SENSE OF THE WORLD

REFLECTION ON KEY CONTEXTS FOR LEARNING:

How are children's everyday experiences visualized?

Do adults model simple ways of thinking about experience – for example, first this happened, then this?

Are ideas routinely 'mapped' in visual ways that demonstrate links between one thing and another?

Is 'choice' presented in clear and visual ways?

How do adults scaffold questions, and do they use simpler question forms first?

How are topics chosen and are adults aware of the difference between visual/sensory content and social content?

How do adults describe and explain social roles and relationships in school, home and community?

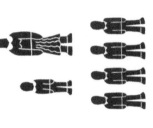

Observing the child in context

LINES OF ENQUIRY ABOUT THE CHILD:

Individual perspectives and ways of making meaning

Existence of strengths and interests

Balance between sensory-perceptual and social ways of making meaning, and changes in this over time

Responses to experience that is visualized, mapped and/or more simply explained

Nature of comments and questions

Methods of observation

A range of methods of observation can be used within educational assessment. Which method we choose is determined partly by what it is we are focusing on, but also by what is feasible in terms of our practitioner role.

1. Participant observation

Participant observation takes place as a natural part of ongoing practice and is the most common form of observation in education. As we engage with pupils, it is possible to note aspects of their behaviour, interaction and communication that are of interest because they form part of a pattern. Participant observations can be planned ahead of time – that is, a decision made to focus on a specific pattern of behaviour as it occurs – or they can be more of a spontaneous 'snapshot' of an interesting aspect of children's experience. What is important to remember is that this is the most natural method of observation, one that provides an overview of contexts for learning and does not intrude on what children are doing. Participant observation allows existing patterns of engagement (or non-engagement) to be seen and children's cultural routines and ordinary issues in communication to be identified, and, for this reason, provides a good starting point for assessment for learning.

In participant observation, the practitioner may be actually involved with pupils and making a mental note of what they do and say, which they jot down at the earliest opportunity. Alternatively, they might record single words and phrases in situ as a mental reminder. They will probably be standing slightly to one side, but in a position where it is possible to hear some of what children say. Children, particularly those who do not have autism, may notice and comment on an adult watching them, and even stop what they are doing. However, regular watching and noting by an adult will mean that children get used to this as a form of practice and eventually cease to notice it in the same way.

Participant observation is helpful in providing information about the quality of pupil experiences and interactions. It is also good for providing information about children and young people's participation and learning that is contextualized and relates to the environment around. Looking at what pupils do can be combined with asking questions to gain further details or to clarify something about what you are seeing. However, watching and listening to children for even a few minutes can result in large amounts of information being gathered and a whole range of issues emerging. It is important to think about how long to observe for and not to observe for too long. An observation that lasts for more than an hour, for example, would almost certainly be too long, and an optimal length of time to observe might actually be much shorter than this.

Observational detail is either remembered and then recorded shortly after the observation or recorded in situ as brief notes, which are then written up in detail afterwards. Remembering is therefore an issue for this method of observation, though the ability to remember the small details of children's activity is a skill that

FIELD NOTE
Date/Time *29 April, 11.20am*
Who is involved *Ella, James, Sonya, Tash*
Where *Outside play area*

Details
This morning James and Ella are playing with the wooden blocks, Ella suggesting that they make a tower using alternate colour blocks. James likes this idea and smiles and flaps his hands every so often. Sonya and Tash look on. No one has instructed her to, but Ella naturally simplifies her language with James, repeating what she says, making the meaning visually clear by pointing and always using James's name first to get his attention.
E: James, blue here (pointing at the tower)
J: (No reply but places blue block)
E: My turn (places block)
J: (No reply but waits)
E: James, white (pointing at the white block and then the tower)
J: (Places white block. Flaps and squeals)
S: Can I have a go? (places blue block)
E: White again (looking straight at James and then pointing at white block)

Figure 2.2 Field note of a participant observation

can be developed. Records of observations can be kept as a running record, diary entries, field notes or dictated notes, and will usually take the form of a narrative account – that is, a detailed description of activity and interaction.

Figure 2.2 is a field note of an observation that concerns the communication experience of James, aged 6, who has a diagnosis of autism, and another girl in his class, Ella, who does not. As she watches James and Ella interact, James's support worker notices that the quality of communication between the two children is particularly good, better it seems to her than James experiences with other pupils in his class. The support worker writes up this 'snapshot' observation, including a snippet of conversation that she has quickly recorded verbatim to provide more detailed evidence, and discusses it with the class teacher. The two practitioners decide to investigate the matter further to see if this kind of exchange occurs as a pattern within James and Ella's interactions, and whether any other children structure their interaction with James in the way that Ella successfully does. They also want to find out more about how these two children, James and Ella, feel about each other to determine whether the encouragement of friendship between them is an appropriate form of support. At this stage, the practitioners feel that both children enjoy interacting with each other, but they want to make sure of this and find out whether Ella's direction of James's activity is ever experienced by him as 'too bossy'.

2. Event sampling

Participant observations use a narrative form of recording that describes all that is happening within a group. They produce a contextualized 'story' of children's

experiences that is recorded as a long sequence of events. Such methods of observation can produce very large amounts of information, which it is sometimes hard
to know how to organize and use within practice. Children's activity is incred-
ibly rich and fast-paced, and even a few minutes of observation will yield many
details about communication, orientation, action, belief, emotion, interaction and
response. There will be occasions when more focused methods of observation will
be needed. This is particularly the case after methods such as participant observation have been used to provide 'the big picture', out of which issues emerge that
are of significance and need further investigation.

Event sampling is a more focused method of observation that investigates a
particular event highlighted in some other way as of significance. It investigates
a short period of time – an event – and so produces information that is focused
and already organized around an issue. Event sampling and time sampling are
similar methods of observation, the latter focusing on the frequency of a selected
behaviour that has been highlighted as important. Time sampling is described
ahead, but it is worth considering that autistic people have a differential experience of 'time', often processing experience at a slower rate and perhaps producing
a delayed – sometimes very delayed – response. It is also the case that children
with autism can be engaged in an activity for very long periods of time – or very
short periods of time – and sampling their activity in a time-based way may produce information that is not that useable.

The experience of autistic pupils in relation to specific events is, by contrast,
something that can be a more worthwhile investigation. Pupils with autism often
have important responses to specific events – for example, the start or end of an
activity or moving from one place to another. In investigating children's experiences of learning, 'positive events' that involve maximum social participation and
communication and 'negative events' that cause distress, withdrawal or overstimu-
lation are equally of interest. The event itself defines what is being observed, and
the occurrence of the event prompts focused investigation into the experience of
all children or young people and adults involved. An event can be of any length of
time, but it is a good idea to have some time limit to avoid the gathering of large
amounts of information. Changes in the duration of an event may be an indicator
of development.

Figure 2.3 provides an example of event sampling for a girl, Kelly, aged 6, who
is autistic. Kelly is often tearful after playtimes, and this has been highlighted as
a significant event that seems to occur as a pattern even on days when she is
happy and settled. Triggers for the behaviour are not clear, and Kelly's teacher
and support worker decide that when this event occurs they will investigate what
happened just before the tearfulness, what was said and done by all the people
involved with Kelly and what was the sequence of 'mini-events' within this event
unit. All practitioners involved with Kelly are alerted to the fact that tearfulness
may occur and that they should begin systematic observation when they notice
conflict or any other kind of upset occurring at playtimes. After carrying out two

Event: *Tearfulness following outside play*

Date/Time	Duration	Who is involved	Details
Tues 26 11.10am	30 mins	Kelly, Aesha, Tom	K was extremely upset and cried uncontrollably for 10+ mins. She wasn't able to speak. A said K had grabbed her bike.
Fri 29 11am	20 mins	Kelly, Alex	K hit A with bat. They had been playing jumbo tennis. K cried and said, 'Home time' over and over again.
Mon 1 10.50am	1 hr	Kelly, Elliot, Sam, Aesha	Children playing on bikes- lots of arguments. K crying and upset for rest of day.

Analysis: *Incidents are happening during mornings when more equipment is available outside – play involves more movement in the yard. Kelly enjoys going on back of tandem bike, but has to wait her turn.*

Figure 2.3 Event sampling record

weeks of focused investigation, practitioners analyse their records to see if there is a pattern in relation to Kelly's tearfulness. They note that incidents occur mostly in the mornings, when the bikes and other equipment are available at playtimes, and that Kelly becomes more anxious and distressed when she has to share the equipment or wait her turn. They note too that the presence of the equipment means faster movement and more collisions in the playground. The decision is made to support Kelly in being able to take turns by introducing a rota for the bikes and time-limiting children's turns on the bikes. A 'road system' is marked out as lines on the playground to organize the movement of the bikes since all children struggle with the number of crashes and collisions. In follow-up observations, it is noted that tearfulness for Kelly occurs less frequently, and that when it does occur, the duration of upset is for a much shorter period of time.

3. Ecological observation

Ecological observation is a naturalistic form of observation that pays attention to the environmental influences on a child's behaviour. Care is taken to record the interactions amongst children and adults as they unfold, noting who begins an interaction, whether another person gets involved and the manner in which they do so. The focus is on the social and cultural activity that takes place within social contexts and the part all individuals play, with the view taken that people cannot be seen as operating outside of this.

Time/Activity 2.05pm/IT lesson	Participation/Interaction	Conversation
Focus Child: Activity/Attention	Ben focused on computer but not following teacher instruction. Spacing out letters on screen and changing them to different fonts, some big, some small. Cheers as he does this	
Initiation/Role	Ben tries to direct attention of boys nearby, pointing at his screen	
Partner no. 1 Activity/Attention/ Role	Sam is concerned that Ben is not following lesson and tries to stop him. Glances nervously at teacher	'No, that's not what we're doing', deleting letters on Ben's screen. Ben resists Sam, pushing him away
Further partners: No. 2	Thomas glances over at Ben's screen but then looks back at his own	
No. 3	Lee, furthest away, does not notice Ben	
Location/Seating arrangement Teacher activity Environment	Field notes: IT Suite: Ben, Sam, Thomas and Lee are sitting in a line, each at a computer and with their backs to the teacher. Teacher is mostly on other side of room. Sam sits beside Ben, who is next to window. Class settled and quiet	

Figure 2.4 Ecological observation schedule (adapted from Tudge and Hogan, 2005)

Figure 2.4 provides an example of an ecological record of the participation of an autistic boy, Ben, aged 8, and his small peer group, who are mostly boys. A brief description of his activity and that of any partners involved with him, as well as the activity of the general class group, is noted to create an ongoing record of how interactions, communication, relationships and roles unfold. This observation of Ben and his peers is part of a series that are carried out by a support worker during the course of an IT lesson. The information gathered shows that Ben's non-involvement in the lesson and fascination with the sensory possibilities of what he can create on his computer screen are a particular source of stress for Sam, the child who is sitting next to him. Sam becomes increasingly angry during the course of the lesson and eventually complains about Ben to other peers, calling him 'stupid' and 'weird'. This pattern of negative interaction between Sam and Ben is picked up by observations at other times of the school day. The class teacher realizes that pairing Ben and Sam is not a good idea and that it is better to suggest Ben sits with other boys in that peer group, who have much less difficulty with the differential way Ben participates in lessons. Sam is also supported in his interactions and friendships since it emerges that he often seeks out Ben to be with and experiences difficulties in relating to other peers.

Records of how pupils engage with each other and with adults – how interaction occurs and the roles that are taken – are all important pieces of information to gather for the purpose of assessment within autism education. The observation schedule shown here is adapted from Tudge and Hogan (2005), who point out that people adopt one of the following social roles within contexts:

- participating;
- facilitating;
- directing;
- resisting or stopping;
- eavesdropping.

Details of social participation, social roles and the ways in which these change over time are important sources of evidence of learning for pupils with autism. Preliminary investigation may need to take place in order to determine who is significant as a child's partner and therefore who needs to be the focus of an ecological observation, but this makes for an observation that is highly relevant socially and provides information that is useable in terms of support for learning and social inclusion.

4. Mapping

The way in which an autistic pupil moves around the space can provide extremely useful information when investigated in a focused way. A useful method for doing this is to create a map of the pupil's use of space, whether it is in the classroom, the playground or around the school. During periods of time when the pupil is free to move around – or even during times when they are not but move around anyway – it is possible to note which areas of the space they go to and in what order. This gives a picture of what activities the pupil is seeking out, where they feel most comfortable and what they are not choosing to do. It can provide some insight into how long a pupil is spending somewhere (if timings are also recorded), whether they are 'flitting' from place to place or whether they have a 'safe base' to which they always go back. Maps can be created for different activities, times of the day or parts of the week to show how the child's use of space changes according to these.

In Figure 2.5, it is possible to see the use of space made by a child with autism, Harry, aged 4. This map is completed when Harry has been in the school for only a few weeks and shows his very restricted use of classroom space and preference for looking at books and going on the computer. In observing his use of the space, it is noted by his support worker that it feels as if Harry is 'pacing' between these two areas, with the possibility that this indicates he is experiencing some stress as

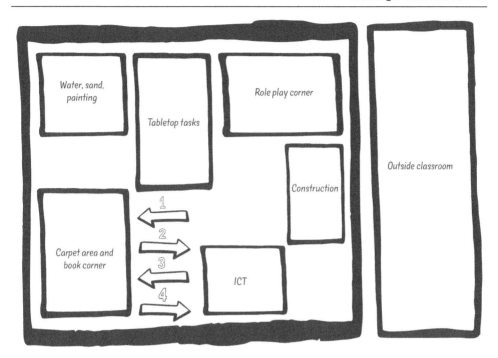

Figure 2.5 Mapping showing a pupil's restricted interests and use of space

a result of being in the classroom. Environmental supports are in place to visually communicate to Harry what is happening now and next, and he is provided with non-social breaks from the classroom throughout the day. There is also a focus on building supportive relationships for Harry, with both adults and one or two pupils. When another map is completed several months later, it shows a much wider use of space and engagement in a greater number of activities.

5. Time sampling

Time sampling focuses on the occurrence of behaviour within a time period and is often used to investigate the frequency of behaviour. Time sampling is a highly formal method of observation that requires the practitioner to be specific in terms of when and where to observe, and at what intervals to record the incidence of behaviour. It has the benefit of providing information that is precise, detailed and limited, and provides a contrasting method to participant observation, for example, which is more open-ended.

Figure 2.6 provides an example of a time sampling record that is used to investigate the communication of a child with autism, Millie, aged 6. Through participant observation, Millie's class teacher has noticed that Millie uses more

Child:		Millie		Date:	4 October
Time period:		30 minutes		Activity:	Free play

Time	Who is involved	Behaviour(s):		Comment:
		Verbal communication	Non-verbal communication	
9.00				No communication – drawing
9.05	M + Jay		✓	Shows picture to neighbor
9.10				No communication – drawing
9.15	M + Jay		✓	J comments on picture, M nods
9.20	M + Leroy		✓	M playing with windmills. L snatches, M takes back and looks angrily at him, vocalising
9.25	M + Leroy	✓		M tells L to go away
9.30	M + Sally		✓	M + S have windmill each. M looks and follows S when she spins it, and laughs with her

Figure 2.6 Time sampling schedule

non-verbal communication in her interactions with peers. She wants to gather detailed information about this issue, which is an important one for Millie, and decides to investigate the frequency of non-verbal and verbal communication. The class teacher chooses to observe at five-minute intervals for half an hour, looking for a 30-second window each time and recording a tick if she sees any evidence of verbal and non-verbal behaviour. She thinks about what she means by non-verbal communication and defines it as any use of gesture or eye contact by Millie, her body co-ordination to a peer, her use of touch and any socially shared facial expression or expression of emotion.

This observation and observations carried out on subsequent days that week show that Millie is relying mostly on non-verbal communication, though she uses verbal communication when the communication situation becomes more difficult. It is apparent that Millie's experience of verbal communication involves greater experiences of negative emotion, and her class teacher makes a request that a communication group is provided. This provides playful and enjoyable experiences of call-and-response activities and other simple verbal games to give Millie a more positive experience of verbal communication.

Time sampling is a good method to use where behaviour can be defined and is clearly visible, and lends itself to the quantification of behaviour. Quantifying behaviour provides a clear form of measurement and is therefore useful when assessing pupils' attainment and demonstrating progress. For this reason, quantifying behaviour is a method of investigation that has been privileged within autism education and is sometimes put forward as the only method of assessment that can be used. However, some caution is necessary in relation to methods that quantify behaviour only, especially in relation to the behaviour of an autistic pupil. Many important lines of investigation within autism education involve processes in social cognition and emotion that are not easily defined and not visible. In looking at children's engagement with each other and the social environment, it is crucially important to know about their social understandings, interpretations and motivations, their experiences of relationships, intimacy and pleasure, and their experiences of participation, cooperation and support. However, none of these areas are easily measured and many cannot be quantified.

The complexity of social experience means that it is also easy to misjudge whether a behaviour is significant and therefore needs to be measured. A good example of this in autism theory and practice is the wide use of 'social initiation' as an indication of social engagement and therefore something to be counted. In children's social worlds repeated requests to play or be a friend can be perceived as inappropriate by other children and lead to negative judgements and social rejection. The autistic pupil who makes repeated requests for social interaction might achieve a high rating when assessed against the criteria of 'social initiation', yet actually be experiencing social failure. It is much better to use methods that provide information about the quality of experience in these instances and how a child's behaviour relates to the context in which it occurs, which includes the behaviours, attitudes, understandings and practices of other people.

Following up on an observation

Observation is a tool within educational practice, and it is important to make full use of an observation by following it up once it has been carried out. After an observation it is important to:

- analyse your findings in light of the aim of the observation and by comparing them with information from other sources – for example, other people's observations, conversations with children and parents;
- identify experiences of learning – for example, by looking for cultural routines and patterns of social engagement. Decide on next steps in learning and plan new teaching;

- identify learning needs – for example, by looking at patterns of challenge – and plan learning supports;
- decide if there are any issues that need more focused investigation.

It is also important to think about your practice, policy and ethics in relation to the way observations are carried out and used within your setting. In order for observation to remain effective as a tool it is worth evaluating practice on a regular basis with the staff group. The questions set out in Table 2.1 can be used for the purpose of evaluation.

Table 2.1 Evaluation of observation practice

Questions for reflection	Comment
What types of observation are most commonly carried out in your setting? What are typical aims of observations and how are they identified? Do you need to make observations for other purposes?	
Which pupils are observed most? How sensitively are observations carried out? Do pupils ever experience them as intrusive and are they allowed to indicate that they do not want to be observed?	
What arrangements exist for sharing observations: • between practitioners? • between practitioners and pupils? • between practitioners and parents?	
What do you do with observational material once it has been reviewed? How, where and for what length of time is it stored?	
How are practitioners supported in relation to making observations? How are new practitioners informed about observational practice in your setting? What aspects of observational practice would you like to develop?	

Chapter 3

Listening to children

Focus of this chapter:

- listening to children as an approach to teaching and learning within inclusive education
- adapting methods of listening to children for the purpose of listening within inclusive autism education
- developing tools for listening, including open and closed questions, ranking, conversation mind maps and role play
- working through parent partnerships.

Introduction

The agenda of listening to children and including 'the voice of the child' in planning and evaluation of provision is being seen as an increasingly important one. Our understanding that children have rights on a par with adults to be consulted on matters that affect them has been influenced by a range of government guidance and agreements, most notably the UN Convention on the Rights of the Child (UN General Assembly, 1989). This international treaty requires signatories to take children's views seriously and to actively seek them out. It sees even the most vulnerable children as capable of forming an opinion and having the right to be consulted.

The traditional view of children has been that they are underdeveloped, not yet fully formed or capable and so unreliable as informants. However, recent theorizing in childhood studies about 'what is a child' puts forward the idea that children are social actors who actively participate in and make sense of their everyday experiences (James et al., 1998). Children have competencies, both in their social interactions and in their ability to reflect on these (Woodhead and Faulkner, 2008). They actively make sense of and develop beliefs about themselves and the world with which they engage, and so have unique information about their lives. It is the responsibility of adults to find a way of accessing this, by identifying appropriate methods for listening to children and by creating tools that enable children to share their views in ways adults can understand. Children are seen as a diverse group with different levels of skill and different competencies (Christensen and James, 2008). Adults must work harder, therefore, to listen to some children, but all children should be seen as competent and as having a voice.

The voice of the autistic child

Despite this agenda of listening, the voice of the autistic child is notable in its absence. Some theorists have argued that being autistic precludes a person from having insight into their own experience. Autism has been conceptualised as the lack of 'an experiencing self' – that is, a sense of self in relation to everyday perceptions and interactions, one that is able to recall and reflect upon experience (Frith and Happé, 1999; Jordan and Powell, 1995). Traditionally in the field of autism, research has been seen as needing to find methods that do not rely on 'voice'. Nevertheless, research studies do exist which investigate the views of autistic people about their everyday experiences, and which include personal insights, individual meanings about social interactions, and reflections on concrete as well as ideational aspects of experience (see Beresford et al., 2004; Conn, 2014a; Humphrey and Lewis, 2008; Ochs et al., 2001). It is the case, too, that there are a large number of autobiographies and personal narratives written by autistic adults and children which describe and reflect on the experience of autism in rich and powerful ways. Increasingly, it is understood within the helping professions that personal narratives are an important way of giving voice to service users and guiding the practice of professionals (Billington, 2006).

For those of us who seek to support children and young people in their communication and everyday interactions, gaining their perspectives on their everyday experiences is an essential process in knowing how to provide learning support. Interaction – with other people and with the environment – involves motivation, emotion and an unfolding personal experience, and none of these things are straightforwardly known by a person who is outside of that interaction. Two or three children's experience of each other, the amount of enjoyment or frustration involved in their social relations, the way in which they understand or do not understand each other, and their investment to pursue further social contact are experiences that are not easily known outside of that small group. Autism practitioners are most interested in children's and young people's social relationships and social communication, and seek to support these areas of learning. Understanding all children's and young people's perspectives on social experiences – listening to autistic pupils, but also to the peers who know them – provides a way forward in this respect.

In listening to children, adults are often described as needing to pay very close attention to the child's ways of making sense and to 'tune in' to their communication (Westcott and Littleton, 2005). The adult must engage in a process that is conceived of as intersubjective engagement, where they align their subjectivity to that of the child, using their experience and knowledge as a human being to imagine their way into and *share* the child's point of view. Intersubjectivity is an extremely rich form of interpersonal sharing, but it could not be said to apply straightforwardly to autistic-neurotypical interactions. The autistic child's sensory and partly non-social ways of making meaning must be seen as a challenge to the neurotypical adult knowing about, understanding and being able to intersubjectively share. Adults may have to accept that they may not be able to understand fully the autistic child's individualistic subjectivity, but this should not be seen as an argument against seeking children's and young people's views and gathering information about their experiences.

Listening to children as an educational approach

Listening to children is a practice that exists within education as a method of evaluation of teaching and learning and as a pedagogical approach to enrich pupil learning. Teachers routinely ask pupils about what they know and show an interest in how they have engaged with learning. Listening to children is envisaged as an important way of supporting them to think about their learning and reflect on their engagement with learning processes. It is a feature of reflective practice which views learning as located within the learner. The role of the reflective teacher is one of finding out about the pupil's experiences of learning as a way of being able to support them, to 'scaffold' their learning and to move them on in terms of development. Reflective teaching is described as 'a pedagogy of listening and relationship' (Clark, 2005) where teachers build supportive relationships, explore pupils' interactions with their environment and each other, and use different forms of listening to support learning and development. In reflective teaching, the teacher takes a non-didactic role and follows the pupil's lead, making investigations of their ways of making meaning, usually within natural contexts.

For pupils with special educational needs and disability, gaining their voice within evaluations of teaching and learning is also seen as educationally important (DfE/DoH, 2015). Alongside parents and practitioners, pupils are invited to participate in reviews of special provision and the identification of learning targets. They may be consulted about what they see as important in their development or they may be asked for their views on their attainments and progress.

In education, different modes of listening are seen as possible. Children are viewed as interacting with the world in multimodal ways, through verbal communication but, probably more importantly, through a range of non-verbal modes too. Observation is viewed as a key method of listening to children and seeing communication that takes place – for example, as gesture, movement, sound, body posture and gaze. Alternative methods to observation are also available, which include talking to pupils and asking them questions, talking to adults who know them, asking pupils to represent their experience in drawings and photographs, and asking them to re-enact their experience or show it in some other way.

Adapting methods for listening to autistic pupils

Listening to children is envisaged as involving the creative development of 'tools for listening', ones that enable children to understand what is being asked of them, to reflect on their experience and to share their thoughts and opinions. Listening to autistic children means that we might have to work harder to do this. Methods of listening will probably have to be adjusted and innovative ways of supporting children's reflective engagement found, and the following key processes are ones to keep in mind.

Asking focused questions

When listening to children it is important to ask concrete and specific questions, and pay close attention to the way in which questions are framed. This is particularly the case for autistic pupils, for whom questions such as 'Who do you play with?' or 'What games do you play?' are probably too non-specific and may give rise to answers that relate more to the context in which the question is asked than to their everyday experience. It will be important to ask focused questions that emerge from investigations using other methods into the child's or young person's lived experience. Observations of children playing and conversations with parents and other adults will give specific details about their playmates, preferred activities, forms of play, friendship experiences, social interests and social difficulties. Questions can then be asked specifically about these as a way of gaining an understanding of the pupil's experience. Questions such as 'Show me what you do when you play ___', naming a game that you know is favoured by the pupil, and 'What do you do with ___?', naming a peer with whom you know the pupil regularly associates, can provide valuable insight into the quality of social experience for a child. Examples of topics for questions are:

- 'My favourite games';
- 'I like it when . . . ';
- 'People I understand';
- 'Me and my friends';
- 'People who help me'.

Using tools for 'visible listening'

It is important to provide visual supports in conversations with children and young people. Again, this is particularly the case for autistic pupils, who have a greater need for language to be presented in alternative modes, not just as the spoken word. It is helpful to think about listening to autistic pupils as a kind of 'visible listening' (Clark and Moss, 2011), where what is being talked about is always visualized in some way. Children can be asked to show, act out, refer to pictures and symbols, point to objects, look at photographs, sequence pictures and map out their ideas on paper.

Visual information is a way both of communicating with children and of children communicating their ideas to you, but some caution is necessary. Methods for listening to children typically use children's drawings of their play spaces, friends and interests, or children are given cameras to take photographs of what is important to them. Such an approach relies on the adult making interpretations of what the child is representing about their experience in their drawing or photograph. As discussed earlier, the individualistic subjectivity that operates in autism means that images produced by autistic children and young people are not necessarily open to this kind of analysis. It might be better to think in terms of gaining an overview of a pupil's social engagement, favourite games and patterns of interactions in school, and perhaps at home and in other settings. Once you have established the important cultural routines for the pupil and those with whom they regularly interact, then an adult can take photographs of these. Children are usually happy to be photographed when asked, unless, of course, their activity is in some way open to criticism by an adult! In this way, photographs that are socially relevant to children's actual lived experience can be obtained and used as the basis for questions addressed to them about that experience. Photographs may be taken of:

- children carrying out a favoured activity, by themselves or with others;
- portrait photographs of children who are friends or potential friends – that is, children who associate with each other regularly or who are on a similar wavelength;
- children playing a favourite game;
- children engaged in an interaction that has been established as part of an interaction pattern or routine – for example, sitting beside each other at lunch, being together in the book corner, or one child watching others when they play.

Gathering information from different sources

The difficulties inherent in interpreting autistic pupils' responses to questions mean that more cross-checking with other sources of information will probably be necessary. This may involve using multiple methods and multiple informants to provide supporting information and add more details about a subject. It will be important to check out other children's experiences of routines, interactions and play. Parents are a vital source of information, since they often hold unique pieces of information about their child and have a greater depth of understanding of their experiences. Other professionals can offer their observations, thoughts and opinions too, to compare and contrast with your own. Of interest are the ways in which children's social activity is perceived, how their communication is received and responded to by others, and the understandings and interests of all those engaged with a pupil.

We listen to children within different contexts, and this influences how we go about the process of listening. We may listen to children in formal ways, as an interview, or we may simply ask questions in situ as pupils go about their everyday activities. The contexts in which we ask questions to some extent determine the nature of children's responses, and it is worthwhile considering the different contexts for listening that are available to educational practitioners and their relative benefits and limitations. Table 3.1 sets out a range of contexts for listening, with the benefits and limitations for listening of each context described.

Table 3.1 Contexts for listening to children

In situ	Asking pupils questions in situ as they go about ordinary interaction and play can be done during an observation: • to check out a detail with children – for example, 'What did you just say to him?' • to get more information about interaction – for example, 'Whose idea was this?' *Benefits:* This is a very concrete form of listening that allows you to refer to features of a pupil's actual environment. *Limitations:* It interrupts children's play and interactions and may bring them to an end.
One-to-one conversations	Can be carried out informally whilst engaged in an activity with a pupil, or more formally as an interview. Your relationship with the pupil will be of significance. *Benefits:* Formal interviews can be planned beforehand and supported with a visual schedule and other visual tools. *Limitations:* The pupil may not understand the meaning of an interview-type situation and that questions relate to their experience outside of the conversation.
Within a pair or group	Pupils can be asked questions within their ordinary friendship groups: • as part of a focus group • using drama and role play • as a way of including all peers. *Benefits:* Asking children as a group will give insight into group dynamics in everyday life. *Limitations:* Children are sensitive to each other's presence and some might dominate the group.

Practitioner conversations	Communication is a key aspect of working in inclusive autism education, not only communicating with children and young people but also establishing effective communication with other professionals. *Benefits:* Sharing ideas can minimise wrong assumptions about the meaning of pupils' behaviour. *Limitations:* Finding time to liaise is often difficult for educational practitioners.
Parent partnerships	Parents hold unique information about their child. Two-way listening is important not only so that parents are informed about their child's education but also so that they are allowed to share their views. *Benefits:* Parents often achieve a deep understanding of their child's behaviour. *Limitations:* If parents are questioned with their child, they may answer for them.
The sensory environment	'Tuning in' to the pupil's sensory experience is a critical form of listening to children. Carrying out this type of investigation can be supported by using a sensory audit. *Benefits:* Sensory experiences are key experiences for autistic pupils and will constitute strong influences on behaviour. *Limitations:* The autistic pupil's non-social, sensory experience of the world is hard for neurotypical adults to 'see' and understand.
Written communication	Some children and young people with autism respond well to questions that are written down, to which they can also supply written answers. This allows them to avoid face-to-face interaction, which many autistic people find stressful. *Benefits:* For some people with autism, written communication is more comfortable than verbal communication. *Limitations:* Written communication provides less opportunity for flexibility in communication – for example, asking for clarification.
Online	Communicating via computers is thought by some to be the most natural form of communication for autistic people. Pupils can communicate with their teacher by email and can respond to questions provided in an online questionnaire. *Benefits:* Online communication is a form of communication that avoids face-to-face interactions. *Limitations:* Non-autistic professionals may have to overcome a personal dislike of communicating online.

Developing tools for listening to children

When listening to autistic pupils there is the very real possibility that what is being expressed by the child is not social but sensory experience. For many autistic people, sensory experience is paramount but is non-social and does not relate to understandings gained from the social world and from social relationships. A room in a school, for example, may not be perceived and understood as a 'classroom' with all the social expectations, norms and routines that would automatically follow from this. Rather, it may be experienced in terms of sounds heard, shapes and colours seen, patterns of movement or events that occur, and the way in which these are configured at the moment of perception. Non-social sensory experience is individualistically experienced in ways that are not that shareable with other people. For neurotypical people, non-social sensory experience can feel unusual and fascinating, but also strange and unknowable.

People with autism can experience a range of differences in terms of perception and sensory processing. They may be hypersensitive to sensory stimuli and so 'over-aroused' and avoidant of sensory experience, or they may be hyposensitive and experience low arousal so that they constantly seek out sensory stimulation. There may be fluctuation between these two states and, in addition to this, an experience of fragmented perception, where only parts of objects are seen. People may be perceived in a distorted way, with only parts of the body and face perceived, or their presence may be processed across sensory modalities – that is, perceived with an aura of colour or shape (Bogdashina, 2003; Gerland, 1997). Writers with autism describe differential ways of processing sensory-perceptual experience that involve, for example, confusion about the precise location and nature of the experience. In an interview with Cesaroni and Garber (1991), Jim, an adult with autism, powerfully describes his special sensitivity to touch, particularly touch on his face. He describes an experience of confusion not only about where he is being touched but also about 'crossed lines' in terms of the sensory modality – touch on his lower face, for example, producing a sound-like sensation.

For many autistic people, the experience of their sensory world can be one of intense pleasure, but it is highly individualistic as an experience and does not tend to give rise to shared understandings and shared cultural practices. Children with autism may explore less and not seek out shared meanings with others, turning away from new situations. Unlike neurotypical children, who seek out novelty and the differences between things, the preference of children with autism is for sameness, and for experience that is 'locally coherent' (Straus, 2013). Listening to autistic pupils involves an acceptance of this: that we as adults cannot necessarily 'work it out', however hard we try. Investigating the autistic pupil's sensory experience of school may help us to achieve a little more understanding. Though non-social sensory experience, by definition, is individualistic in nature, patterns of experience do exist and the questions set out in Table 3.2, which concern the pupil's sensory experience, provide a useful starting point for listening to autistic pupils.

In gathering pupils' views, it is important to create 'tools for listening' that enable pupils to participate in consultations about their social experiences in school and express themselves. Children have differing abilities, but many can engage with what is being asked of them if communication is clear, concrete and visually systematic. What follows is a description of tools for listening that are particularly suitable for use with autistic pupils and allow them to describe their social and emotional experiences.

Table 3.2 Framing questions about the pupil's sensory environment

Sight	*Does the pupil:*
	• seek out light sources or reflected light *or* dislike light?
	• look between their fingers?
	• seem to fear *or* be fascinated by flashing light?
	• look at the minute details of objects?
	• find it difficult to go down stairs?
	• respond differently to different colours?
	• seem startled when another person suddenly approaches?
Sound	*Does the pupil:*
	• cover their ears?
	• find it hard to concentrate in a noisy environment?
	• make a constant noise – for example, humming or tapping?
	• have acute hearing *or* appear deaf at times?
	• tune in to distant sounds and conversations?
	• fear certain noises *or* seek out certain noises?
Touch	*Does the pupil:*
	• avoid touching messy, gooey or sticky substances?
	• resist being touched *or* seek out touch?
	• enjoy being hugged tightly?
	• find it hard to tolerate certain foods, clothes or events, such as haircuts?
	• have a fascination for certain textures or shapes?
	• hit themselves hard but not seem to feel it?
Smell/Taste	*Does the pupil:*
	• feel disgusted by certain smells *or* seek out smell?
	• sniff things?
	• insist on wearing the same clothes?
	• have difficulties with eating a range of foods, or eat only one food type?
	• take tiny bites when eating?
	• dislike foods that have been mixed together?
Body sense	*Does the pupil:*
	• delight in some motor movement – for example, bouncing, spinning?
	• like to wrap themselves up tightly and burrow under things?
	• lean against people or objects, have difficulty sitting on the floor and appear to be 'floppy'?
	• walk on their tiptoes?
	• appear not to know when they are hot, cold, hungry, need to go to the toilet?
	• seem unable to distinguish between light and hard touch?

1. Open and closed questions

Framing questions that are meaningful to children and young people and effective in gathering their views is not a simple question-and-answer process. Asking questions involves children making sense of what is being asked – and the context in which it is being asked – and coming up with appropriate responses. It is important for adults to consider the way in which questions are asked and the sensitivity of what they are asking about. A question such as 'Who are your friends?', for example, might elicit a list of names from a child who knows that being someone who has friends is an appropriate social identity, even though this may not reflect their own experience. Asking questions involves language, and this means that the language capability of the child needs to be considered. Asking a standard set of questions to all children may not be that effective, and adults need to make judgements about children's individual language capabilities. It is always helpful to use children's own language whenever possible – for example, their names for games or ways of describing their peers. Sometimes it is helpful to ask questions within pairs or small groups since this can feel more natural to children, though children's answers may then reflect the dynamic that exists within that group.

Language will be an issue when asking questions of autistic pupils, and consideration needs to be given to how questions are framed. Questions will probably need to be phrased carefully, using simple but precise language. The context in which questions are asked is important. For example, asking a question such as 'What do you like to play?' may elicit a response from a pupil that relates to play they carry out in the space where the question is being asked, or to somewhere nearby, but not to a more generalized experience of play. Asking the question 'What do you play here?', showing a photograph of a particular space, may be a much more effective approach. It is also helpful to refer to concrete rather than abstract social processes, though some children with autism will be more able in this respect (Beresford et al., 2004). Asking questions in situ as pupils go about their interactions and play, gently and politely enquiring about what someone has just said or done, can provide useful detail.

It is important to think in terms of 'closed' and 'open' questions. A closed question is one that elicits a yes or no answer, or a specific piece of information. Examples of closed questions are 'Do you like to play chase at playtimes?', 'Is the computer your favourite activity?' and 'Who are your friends?' By contrast, an open-ended question is one that requires more than a one-word answer and that opens up a conversation. Examples of open-ended questions are 'What is your favourite thing to do in school?', 'What do you do in the play corner?' and 'Can you describe ___ ?', showing a picture of a friend. Harrington et al. (2013) found in their study that asking a closed question to begin with and then following this up with open-ended questions was an effective method of listening to autistic children.

Being specific when questioning and knowing what to be concrete about depend on knowing the particular interaction and play routines of the group of pupils with whom you are concerned. Asking questions should take place within a process of progressive focusing, described in Chapter 1 as part of the cycle of assessment for learning. Progressive focusing is where details of the quality of pupils' social relations and interactional experiences are gathered gradually, using different methods. The 'big picture' of all pupil activity is important as background information about children's 'community practices' (Wenger, 2009) in this setting and how it influences the behaviour, interests and interactions of the individual pupil and smaller groups. Within the process of progressive focusing, pupils' responses can be checked out with other pupils and with adults to compare and contrast information and gain a more detailed picture of the quality of individual and collective experiences within your school community, and the perceived social appropriateness or inappropriateness of pupil participation.

It is always a good idea to ask less sensitive questions first and build up an experience of trust within listening relationships. Adults need to monitor the ways in which pupils respond to questions and how comfortable they are in being questioned. Children are often enthusiastic interviewees, but some subjects may be difficult or even painful for them. Sometimes it is better to asked 'spaced questions' (Beresford, 1997), where a topic is returned to now and again, in between questions about other topics. Asking different questions about the same thing – 'What do you like about playtimes?', 'What do you do not like about playtimes?', 'What do you do by the fence (in the playground)?', 'What happens in Zombie Tag?' (i.e. a game you have observed children playing at playtime) – is a good way of gaining insight into the richness of children's social experiences and perspectives. For some pupils with autism, it is important to give time for questions to be processed and responses to be made. It may be important too to allow the pupil time to go 'off track' and talk about their special interests before bringing them back to the subject about which you are interested (Harrington et al., 2013). Alternatively, you can consult pupils about what questions they think are important to them and ask these, setting them out as a list to be ticked off.

Listening to autistic pupils means that adults will probably have to work harder at interpreting what children and young people say. Shared interpretations between adults and between adults and pupils may be helpful, but supporting questions with visual information is also a good idea. Box 3.1 sets out possible supports for visual listening that can be used with pupils.

Box 3.1   Visual supports for listening

Photographs of people, places and interactions

These will need to be researched beforehand to find out who, what and where is important to the pupil and their peer group, if they have one. The detail in the photo also needs to be carefully considered. A pupil may understand 'Describe ___', naming a peer, game or interaction depicted in the photograph, as a request for them to describe the photo rather than giving a more generalized description of this person, place or event in everyday life.

Asking questions in situ

This allows actual people, places and objects to be referred to when asking questions, and by the pupil when making their responses.

Using objects from everyday life

Enquire about these – for example, 'What do you do with this?' – asking the pupil to show you.

Create puppets using cut-out photographs

These can be manipulated to act out responses to questions.

Using symbols to indicate the subject or subjects under discussion

Symbols can be set out as a visual schedule and removed as each part is discussed. Symbols for 'play', 'talk', 'happy', 'sad', 'by myself' and 'with a friend' may be useful, in addition to symbols for 'feel', 'hear', 'see', 'smell' and so on.

Ways of using visual information are explored in more depth in the following pages. What is important to remember is the relative level of difficulty of question forms. 'What' and 'who' questions are more straightforward than 'why' questions, and the phrasing of questions is important. Autistic children often respond well to simple sequencing – for example, 'then what happens . . . and then . . . ?', or 'what happens first . . . what happens next . . . ?' This can be supported by visual information too – for example, putting photographs in a sequence to describe a game or interaction routine. Table 3.3 sets out suggestions for framing questions in relation to ordinary areas of pupils' activity.

2. Mapping ideas

Conversations between pupils and practitioners are supported by mapping ideas onto a piece of paper or recording them using digital media. Mapping involves recording ideas about a topic as single words, short phrases or images that are visually organized in some way. Mind maps would be an example of this, where ideas about a central topic are recorded in brief and connected with each other visually, with subgroups relating to these ideas also recorded. It is a good idea to base conversations involving autistic pupils on mapping because it provides

Table 3.3 Framing questions about pupils' experiences in school

Play	Describe ___ *(naming game and/or showing photo)* What happens first in ___? *(naming favourite game)* What happens next? What is ___ doing? *(naming someone and showing photo of game or interaction routine, or asking in situ)* What is ___ saying? Show me what you do with this.
Enjoyment	What do you like? What don't you like? What is your favourite ___? What is your second favourite? Third favourite? Who is funny? What do they do? *(choosing from photos)* Who makes you laugh?
The playground	What do you do here? *(showing photo of an area)* Show me what you do here. Where do you go? Where do you not go? Where is the best place to be by yourself? Where is the best place to be with others/watch others? What do you like in the playground?
Friendship	What games do you like to play with ___? What games do you not like playing? What do you like about ___? Is there anything you don't like? What do you do here? *(asking in situ or showing photo)* Describe ___ *(naming game and asking children in pairs)*
Communication	Who speaks first? Who speaks and who listens? What did you just say to him/her? *(asked as children are interacting with each other)* What do you say when ___? What does he/she say when ___? *(showing photo)*
Sensory experience	What is the noise like? *(in situ and using a noise gauge)* What can you hear? *(in situ or showing a photo)* What can you see? What do you feel when ___? Where do you feel it? Is there a smell? What does ___ feel like?

the pupil with a clear picture of what is being talked about and the connections between different points of discussion. Mapping can be used as a way of visualizing thought and can help pupils make sense of a topic. So useful is mapping to listening to children and young people with autism that several different methods are outlined in this chapter.

Figure 3.1 shows a pyramid map that is used to explore a pupil's experience of social relationships and their views about their social network. The base of the map shows 'people I feel close to' and the upper sections 'people I am less close to' and 'people I am not close to'. Research indicates that the concept of 'closeness', rather than that of the more mentalistic 'companionship', is an important one in friendship for autistic people (Bauminger and Kasari, 2000). Completing a map such as this provides a visual tool for thinking about the experience of friendship for a child, gaining more information about who they feel close to and why. Maps can be filled out over time as the basis for discussion about the changing experience of friendship. However, it is important to remember that the subject of friendship is a very sensitive one for children, including autistic children, and something that needs to be managed carefully by adults. A map of this kind should not be viewed as a straightforward measure of friendship – this child has this many close friends – but more as the basis of a conversation in which the adult tries hard to understand the child's ongoing experience of friendship. For children, friendship is more often a working out of 'am I a friend' rather than a fixed experience (James, 1999). Different categories can be used that may be less sensitive, such as 'people who are fun', 'people who are less fun', 'people who are no fun', 'people I talk to' and 'people I don't understand'.

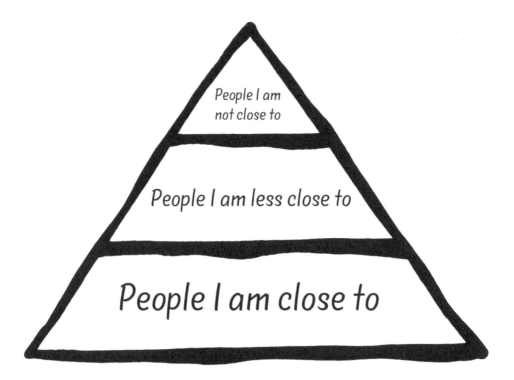

Figure 3.1 Visual map describing a pupil's experience of relationships

Maps can take different shapes. Figure 3.2 shows a concentric map consisting of a series of circles that share a central core. This map records ideas about a topic, in this instance playtimes, with pupils' ideas about playtimes recorded as words or phrases during a brainstorming session. The map is being used as a Thinking Map® (Hyerle and Alper, 2011) to generate ideas to describe a topic. Using a map in this way can be helpful for autistic pupils, who may struggle to generate their own ideas. They may benefit from having access to collective ideas that have been generated by the group, which they can then choose between. Children's experiences are probably closer to each other's than to adult ideas about their experience and will have more authenticity. Generating collective ideas from peers may be an initial stage in thinking about a topic. Ideas that emerge from this stage can then be used by the autistic pupil and their peers to rank or discuss in some other way.

Figure 3.2 Circle map describing a pupil's experience of playtimes (adapted from Hyerle and Alper, 2011)

3. Ranking

Autism involves concrete thinking processes and experiences of the world that are less socially discriminatory and nuanced. Children and young people with autism often describe their social experiences in straightforward 'black and white' terms. They may find it hard to see small social differences between experiences and the feelings that relate to these. Sometimes it is helpful to translate social experience into a visual system of ranking – for example, using numbers to organize levels of experience. The Incredible 5-Point Scale (Buron and Curtis, 2012) is a good example of such an approach that uses the relative strength autistic people have in systematic thinking. The 5-Point Scale uses number and colour to help pupils understand social experience, but other forms of ranking are possible. Figure 3.3 provides a range of methods of ranking that vary in complexity. Experience can be ranked simply as good or bad, but it can also be presented with more complexity, such as 'neither good nor bad, but just okay'. Where a wider range of categories are used, pupils may need support to think about what those categories mean for them, and what the differences are between one level of experience and the next

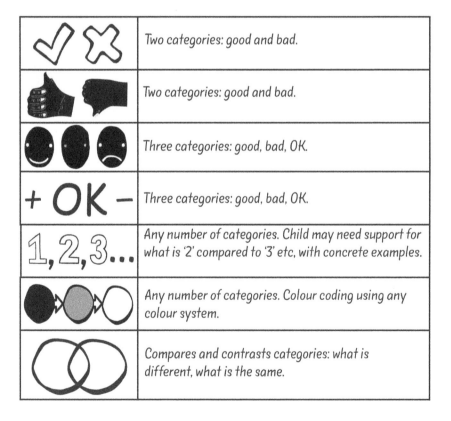

✓ ✗	Two categories: good and bad.
👍 👎	Two categories: good and bad.
☺ ☹	Three categories: good, bad, OK.
+ OK −	Three categories: good, bad, OK.
1, 2, 3...	Any number of categories. Child may need support for what is '2' compared to '3' etc, with concrete examples.
	Any number of categories. Colour coding using any colour system.
⊕	Compares and contrasts categories: what is different, what is the same.

Figure 3.3 Examples of visual systems of ranking

identified level. Concrete examples from children's real-life experiences can be used for this purpose.

Ranking is an activity that can be used within individual conversations with pupils, but also within groups. Pupils can be asked as a group to rate their experience according to ranks. A 'value line' (Shephard and Treseder, 2002) is a useful method to use with groups to gain information about how children see themselves within the group. This is a line marked out on the floor which has two clear poles – for example, 'I agree' at one end and 'I disagree' at the other. A statement is made, and children are asked to describe themselves or their experience by positioning themselves on the line. A statement might be read such as 'I play with equipment in the playground more than I play imaginative games', and pupils position themselves on the line according to whether they agree or do not agree. An alternative way of using a value line is to demarcate it into '1, 2, 3', with '1' and '3' at either end to designate opposing positions and '2' in the middle to designate a 'sometimes' position (see Figure 3.4). Statements are read out, and pupils position themselves according to whether they do or do not do something, or sometimes do it. An example of this use of a value line is reading the statement 'I enjoy playing ___', naming a specific game that children in the group play. Pupils then position themselves on a line that has been marked 'All the time', 'Sometimes' and 'Never'.

It is important that statements be socially relevant to your setting and refer to the actual experiences of children. If children do not play sporty games, for example, or equipment for such play is not available in the playground, then a statement relating to sport should not be included. Asking pupils questions about their play and interactions will need to follow investigation into the specific play cultures in your setting. It is these that inform your ideas about questions and will be more useful than predetermined questions about play and interaction. Examples of statements for value lines would be:

Figure 3.4 Pupils organize themselves on a value line marked 1, 2 and 3, according to which statement best describes them (adapted from Shephard and Treseder, 2002)

- 'I play sporty games' – 'I play mostly pretend games' – 'I like to chat with my friends';
- 'I have lots of ideas and like to be a leader in play' – 'Sometimes I lead and sometimes I listen' – 'I like to listen and follow other people';
- 'I like to be on my own' – 'Sometimes I like to be with people' – 'I always want to be with people'.

Groups should consist of pupils who know each other and are part of an existing peer network. Asking questions within a group results in responses that describe how children wish to be identified within that group and the dynamics that exist in everyday life. This is important information in itself, but may need to be complemented with other ways of listening to children.

4. Good day, bad day

A straightforward way of thinking about and sharing everyday experience is to use the concept of a 'good day' and a 'bad day'. These concepts are meaningfully used with very young children (Clark, 2005) and within strategies for person-centred planning (Sanderson and Lewis, 2012). Those of us who support autistic pupils will know that the idea of 'good days' and 'bad days' is a very natural way of describing their experience too. There is a 'black and white' quality that suits the experience of autism. It also describes the cumulative experience of stress in autism, where stress builds as the result of small triggers occurring over a period of time and the state of being stressed is a longer-lasting one. Parents and teachers of autistic pupils often describe them as having good and bad days, and it may be helpful to think about what makes a good day and what makes a bad day for a pupil. Ideas from children and adults can be recorded under two categories which are visually organized into 'Good day' and 'Bad day' as a visual mapping exercise (see Figure 3.5).

5. Conversation mind maps

There is considerable overlap in the methods used to listen to children in education and methods used in child-centred research, particularly within the field of childhood studies – for example, research methods used with autistic children often advocate the use of systems of communication found in education as a way of structuring research interviews (Beresford et al., 2004; Preece and Jordan, 2009). A conversation mind map is a method used in child-centred research that is highly applicable to supporting autistic pupils in schools to reflect on their social and learning experiences. Conversation mind maps have been used in research with disabled teenagers who use augmentative and alternative communication (Wickenden, 2010) and involve writing out a conversation on paper as an alternative to using voice. Questions, answers and comments are written down rather than spoken and organized around the central image of the topic, which may

Figure 3.5 Template for recording descriptions of a good and bad day at school

include 'important people', 'things I love and hate', 'people who help me' and 'my ways of talking'. Written forms of communication can be much more accessible to some autistic children and adults, especially those who find writing down their thoughts a slower, more permanent and less socially demanding exercise than verbalising them. As with other ways of asking questions, focusing on less sensitive topics first, asking the same question in different ways, revisiting topics and reflecting on previous responses are all important techniques to consider. Figure 3.6 depicts a conversation mind map with topics that have been numbered by the pupil in the order in which they want to write about them.

Beresford et al. (2007) use a similar method to investigate what is valued by autistic children in their lives. Their interviews with children were supported by a mind map of the child's life, which included images for topics on health and comfort, activities and experience, school, emotions, the child's understanding of their autism, how people viewed them, communicating, and relationships with other children. As children spoke about each topic, these were crossed off on the mind map to structure the child's experience of the interview.

6. Storyboarding

Finding ways of visually representing social experience and of describing it in sequence can provide a meaningful reflective approach for autistic pupils. Comic strip conversations (Gray, 1994) is a support strategy that uses this approach by visually representing and 'concretizing' complex social processes as stick figures, symbols, speech bubbles and thought bubbles. Presenting human experience as a series of pictures and concrete images comes close to what Temple Grandin, the well-known professor of animal science and autistic writer, famously described as her experience of the world. In her book *Thinking in Pictures* (Grandin, 2006), Grandin describes her experience of thought as one of watching a series of moving three-dimensional images that is similar to watching a film. She writes that she is able to stop, start and rewind thought in the way it is possible to control film, and describes how she visualizes abstract concepts as concrete images or symbols, which she then combines or manipulates to create meaning.

Storyboarding is a reflective approach that uses the idea of life as a film. A storyboard is used to plan a film by structuring it as image, dialogue and sound. Using a storyboard to talk to pupils about their real-life experience provides a structured way of thinking about and describing that experience. Within conversations with pupils, the child or the adult might draw out a sequence of events in response to the question 'What happens when . . . and then what happens?', recording the different components of experience separately – that is, what people do, what they say, how they might feel and any sensory experience (see Figure 3.7).

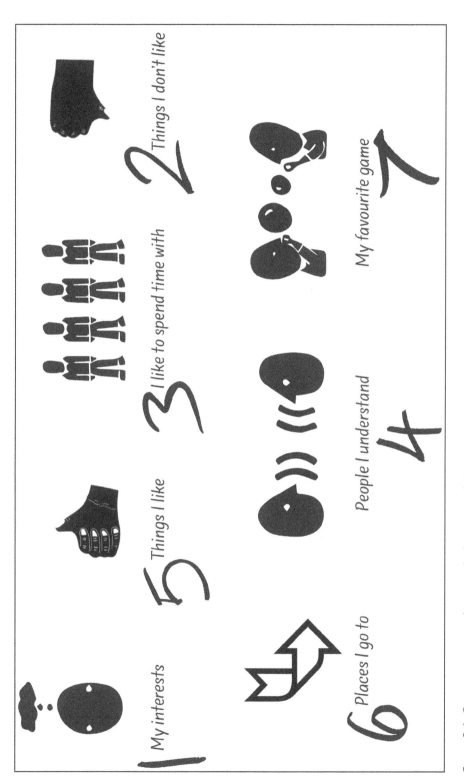

Figure 3.6 Conversation mind map with the order of discussion marked numerically (adapted from Wickenden, 2010)

ACTION	ACTION	ACTION
DIALOGUE	DIALOGUE	DIALOGUE
EMOTION	EMOTION	EMOTION
SPECIAL FX	SPECIAL FX	SPECIAL FX

Figure 3.7 Template for a three-part storyboard

7. Role play

Drama provides a unique opportunity for children to represent and explore their real-life social experiences. Using dramatic techniques, such as role play, scene creation and scripting, it is possible for drama to support the visualization of experience and make it available for discussion. Veale (2005) describes drama as a kind of reverse process to Vygotsky's concept of internalization of social experience, which he argued was the basis of development of human cognition. As Veale describes it, participating in dramatic re-enactment of real-life situations essentially puts the original experience 'back out there'. Drama pares down and simplifies that experience too, by incorporating only significant roles and by freezing the action to focus on aspects of experience. Real life is often too complex an experience for autistic pupils, and methods of slowing down, fixing and replaying aspects of it can provide a valuable tool for listening (Conn, 2007). In this respect, drama may be a more effective tool than, for example, digital video, which produces images that are visually and socially 'dense', just as real life is.

Within a drama group, pupils can take turns to describe their experience of play and interaction. They can be asked to describe a cultural routine, one that you have observed and noted as significant to this group or individual. Their description is then re-enacted by other pupils in the group, who are given specific roles, lines to say and a sequence of actions to perform. Favourite games, conversations, routine interactions and patterns of activity in friendship can all be re-enacted in this way. The pupil who is describing their experience can watch as it is recreated, and then they can be asked to say if there are any inaccuracies in the re-enactment. The group should freeze at significant moments and a discussion should be had about what characters in the scene are thinking and feeling, with all the children in the group contributing to this. It is important to use pupils who actually participate in the play and interaction in real life so that they are able to add details about what goes on from their points of view. It is possible to explore difficult issues within a group in this way – for example, conflicts, negative interactions and problems with friendship – but these are sensitive areas and probably more enjoyable experiences would need to be covered first as a way of building trust in the process.

 Reflective task

Discuss the appropriate methods of listening to gain an understanding of the following:

- the experience of friendship between two children
- teasing of one pupil by a group of their peers
- a pupil's experience of play in the home corner
- a pupil's understanding of verbal communication during the school day.

What methods of observation, if any, would be useful in each case?

Working through parent partnerships

Parents hold unique and valuable information about their child, and professionals must work towards establishing effective partnerships with parents for the purpose of reflection, assessment and planning, and in the evaluation of services. Parents' views about their child's education and the focus for learning will be important, as will insight from parents about family needs, concerns and interests. Since parents have in-depth knowledge of their child, they can also be asked to answer questions about their child's views *as if from their perspective*. Asking parents to put themselves in the place of their child and answer questions as they believe their child would answer can often provide valuable insight into the child's point of view. Questions outlined earlier, in relation to sensory experience, play, enjoyment and experiences of communication, can be addressed to parents of pupils who have little verbal language and those who experience difficulty within verbal interactions.

Chapter 4

Assessment and planning

Focus of this chapter:

- reviewing and analysing information about pupil learning
- making assessments of pupils' attainments in learning
- learning outcomes in relation to the atypical development that occurs for autistic pupils
- the process of identifying SMART targets in relation to specific contexts, learning experiences and support strategies
- demonstrating progress by using the pupil as their own baseline measure.

Introduction

The process of assessment for learning in inclusive autism education is a cyclical one. Information is gathered about the pupil within ordinary contexts, by documenting observations and the outcomes of listening to children and adults. This information is then organized as a way of supporting teacher reflection, assessment and planning. Reviewing and reflecting upon information about children's and young people's learning experiences enable practitioners to identify what is supportive within a pupil's environment, in what ways the pupil has made progress and what are important areas for further learning. Review and reflection also provide practitioners with ideas about how they can support the pupil's next steps in learning – for example, what opportunities exist for developing enabling environments, what learning supports might be required or what adaptations and adjustments need to be made. It is important to recognize what is working well within a pupil's environment, to see what enabling features exist and what strengths and capacities a pupil has, as well as identifying areas of difficulty and exclusion. Often, support for learning is more effective where it values and develops what is already working, rather than looking for what is not working and introducing completely new strategies. The cycle continues with further reflection on new targets set and the pupil's progress in relation to these, with the implementation of support strategies also reviewed and evaluated as part of this process.

The fact that autism is a transactional disability means that barriers to learning exist not only as individual impairment but also in the understandings, values, structures, practices and norms that operate within the child's or young person's social environment. This means that the process of assessment for learning should always take account of the pupil's context as a background to their participation and learning, and not view the pupil as a set of free-floating skills that are uninfluenced by what is going on around. It also means that there needs to be reflection on our own ways of seeing, our values and the judgements we make. For educational practitioners and parents, autism can challenge our fundamental beliefs about children and what they do – for example, that all children enjoy being rewarded or want to have a friend. Effective assessment rests on knowing a pupil well and understanding their points of view, but also on practitioners thinking about what they bring to the assessment situation. As Elwood and Murphy (2015) argue in writing about the nature of sociocultural assessment, it is only by taking account of how and why we are assessing, and what assumptions we are making about pupils, their activity and development, that educational assessment can be fully constructive and equitable.

 Reflective task

Carry out an everyday activity that has been made unusually difficult – for example:

- write a sentence backwards or when looking in a mirror
- walk along a line marked on the floor whilst looking through a pair of binoculars
- open a sealed envelope using tweezers.

Discuss what it felt like to carry out these activities. How did it impact on your sense of self and behaviour? How tiring was it for you?

Think about the pupils you work with and what activities they find difficult and uncomfortable.

Reviewing and analysing information

In reviewing information about pupil participation and learning, it is possible to use different methods for organizing significant pieces of information about their behaviour and activity. Organizing information helps clarify the nature of pupil learning and visualize the significant processes involved in their learning experiences, and so supports teacher reflection.

Visualizing processes of children's learning

Organizing and displaying information about pupils' experience and learning help us to visualize and make sense of the processes that are involved and that are key to their development. Processes involved in children's and young people's learning are often complex, hard to see and highly integrated in terms of cognitive, social, emotional and physical features. By sorting, combining, visually organizing and annotating descriptive pieces of information, it is possible to gain a better understanding of what is going on for a pupil. The process of visualizing children's learning supports shared analysis by practitioners and practitioner-parent conversations.

Capturing actual images of critical moments in learning, when the pupil is taking an active interest and participating effectively, supports conversations with pupils about their learning experiences. Wall displays or one-page stories can be compiled that use images and text to describe significant learning activity in child-friendly form. Reviewing these with pupils supports self-assessment and planning, and provides a powerful source of further learning as pupils review and think about their key experiences in school.

Triangulating information

Combining information from different sources is important for all pupils as a way of making sense of their learning experiences. For autistic pupils, whose behaviour may be harder for others to appreciate and understand, triangulating information is especially relevant. Gathering a range of perspectives – pupil, parent and practitioner – is vitally important to help clarify learning experience and 'work out' what is going on for a pupil in school. External agencies carry out more specialized assessments and may also be invited to contribute to the process of information gathering. Case study 1 illustrates how it is the accumulation of information gained from observation, talking to children and consulting with parents that sheds light on pupil activity – in this instance, a child's act of watching others in play. In this example, the action planning that might have followed from the initial observation of the child's interest in a group of peers is challenged by further evidence gathering and teacher reflection.

Case study 1: Khalil

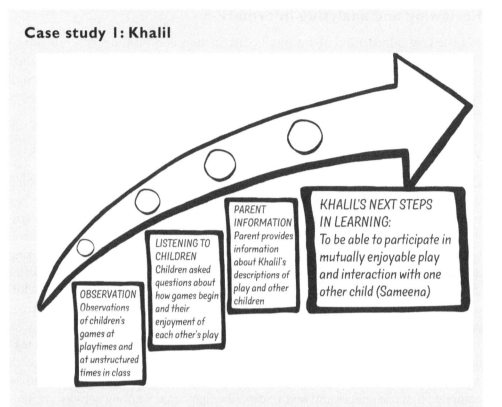

OBSERVATION
Observations
of children's
games at
playtimes and
at unstructured
times in class

LISTENING TO
CHILDREN
Children asked
questions about
how games begin
and their
enjoyment of
each other's play

PARENT
INFORMATION
Parent provides
information
about Khalil's
descriptions of
play and other
children

KHALIL'S NEXT STEPS
IN LEARNING:
To be able to participate in
mutually enjoyable play
and interaction with one
other child (Sameena)

Staff have noticed that Khalil, aged 7, who has a diagnosis of autism, is showing more interest in other children. One particular behaviour they have observed is that he watches the same group of three or four boys who always play super-hero games at playtimes. Staff carry out focused observations of these children and note that, though Khalil stands on the sidelines of these games and watches intently, he is never invited to play by any of these boys. When he does try to join in, interaction quickly develops into a conflict between one of the boys in the group and Khalil, one or another child forcing their ideas on the play. Through participant observation in class, staff have also noticed that Khalil sometimes interacts with a girl in the class, Sameena, who is quiet and shy. From Khalil's parent, they learn that though Khalil often mentions the names of the boys he shows an interest in, he also mentions Sameena's name at home. Staff discuss the fact that the group who plays superhero games is not an inclusive one and comes into conflict with other children or excludes them from activi-ties. On questioning, none of the boys in the group mention Khalil as some-one with whom they enjoyed playing. Staff decide to focus support on Khalil's interactions with Sameena by finding opportunities to pair them for activities, suggesting enjoyable games and putting parents in touch with each other.

Assessment and action planning

When to review a child's progress and make assessments of their learning depends on the purpose of assessment. Teachers carry out formative assessments of children's learning experiences as part of their everyday professional practice, taking steps to find out more about what a child knows and can do as a way of being better able to support further learning within ordinary classroom tasks. Assessment may also take place when the teacher notices that the child has developed in some way and wants to find out more about this. Summative assessments are carried out for more formal reviews of learning – for example, for the purpose of identifying medium- or long-term learning targets or as part of an annual review of progress.

Whether assessment is formative or summative, it will involve making interpretations of children's behaviour and informed judgements about their skills, understanding and knowledge. In making assessments of pupil learning and development, what is of interest is behaviour that is demonstrated on a consistent basis and that occurs regularly enough to constitute a clear pattern of behaviour. Social communication learning is complex, and practitioners should exercise caution about imposing preconceived notions about what is significant in terms of learning behaviour. Practitioners should concern themselves with learning and development across domains, not only certain aspects of communication or social interaction but the full range of communicative, linguistic, social, emotional and physical functioning. Children's learning is embodied, integrated, relational and strongly affective, and all areas of their activity will be of interest.

Carr (2001) makes the important point that children's development has an 'underground' and unknowable quality that makes for unexpected opportunities in learning, ones that have been planned for but also naturally occurring influences that impact powerfully on children's learning. The unknowable nature of learning raises the possibility of wrongly conceived assumptions and judgements by adults of all learners, but perhaps particularly of autistic pupils. Good practice in relation to assessment in autism education involves the practitioner constantly striving to tune in to the pupil and their ways of making sense of the world. Of interest will be the pupil's 'capability set' – that is, their interests and concerns in consideration of external circumstances, supports and opportunities. Being aware of what is important to the pupil and the ways in which their environment enables and extends this, or alternatively puts up barriers, is of central importance within the assessment process.

Review meetings

Part of the assessment process for pupils with special educational needs will involve a formal review meeting which is attended by school practitioners, parents and the multi-professional team. The pupil may also be invited to attend whole or part of the meeting and contribute their viewpoint to the discussion. Prior to the meeting, significant pieces of information that have been gathered in relation to a pupil's recent learning experiences may be distributed for attendees to read and reflect on. During the meeting, these are discussed in order to gain greater insight into the ways in which a pupil is learning and what development is occurring. For a pupil with autism, their social-emotional learning and development will be a key area of discussion, in addition to any academic progress. Table 4.1 provides an example of a review meeting record that includes areas of social-emotional learning particularly relevant to an autistic pupil. These areas of learning are described more fully ahead within the section on learning outcomes, which addresses the atypical development that occurs for many autistic pupils.

Table 4.1 also requires an evaluation of the support that is in place for a pupil. External supports and opportunities, including the understandings, attitudes and actions of others, must always be a consideration in any discussion of a pupil's progress. It is these that help to determine the pupil's experience of difficulty and disability and must be taken into account within any assessment of progress. Clark and Moss (2005) have introduced the idea of reflecting on what to value,

Table 4.1 Review meeting record

Summary of discussion:		Evaluation of support:	
Progress in relation to curriculum areas:		What to value:	
		What to add:	
		What to change:	
Progress in:	*I am able to...*		
Emotional well-being			
Participation		Actions:	*By whom*
Communication			
Making sense of the world			
My next steps in learning are:		**Date of next meeting is:**	

what to add and what to change in terms of experience for children in schools, and Table 4.2 sets out examples of items to value, add and change in the learning experiences of pupils with autism.

Person-centred planning

Increasingly within education, reflection on pupil learning is influenced by methods used in person-centred planning. Person-centred planning was developed in the US and Canada over three decades ago to ensure that the views and experiences of adults with learning disabilities integrally informed processes of planning for their future. Government policy in the UK has advocated the use of person-centred planning with children as a way of valuing them as people and ensuring they have a voice within the planning of their provision (DfE/DoH, 2015; Welsh Government, 2014). For children and young people with autism, person-centred planning is a highly personalized approach that suits their individual needs, though the communication of questions will need to be made clearer and more visual.

Helen Sanderson and others have adapted person-centred planning methods for use in schools, developing tools to support review meetings and the

Table 4.2 Evaluation of learning supports: Examples of items to consider

What to value	**What to add**
For example:	*For example:*
Pupil's special interest	Pupil's name at beginning of sentences
Pupil's interest in others	Visual timetable
Pupil's echolalia	More information visually presented
Interactions with adults	Clear indications of time
Interactions with one other pupil	Concrete experiences
Small groups of peers with which pupil interacts more often	Scripts for specific social contexts
	Colour-coded areas for specific tasks
Inventiveness within sensory play	Motor skills development
Social features of play	

What to change
For example:
Language use by making it simpler
Social breaks to non-social breaks
Seating arrangements – more consideration of seating to one side of the group
Transition arrangements – more consideration of counting down to transition
Sensory aspects of the environment
Staff/pupil levels of knowledge, understanding and attitude
Process of target setting – more involvement of parents

development of action plans (see e.g. Sanderson et al., 2010). A person-centred planning tool that is typically used in school settings is a written record of what is working and not working for a pupil from the perspectives of pupil, the parent and the school. These can be written up as posters in a large-scale format and displayed on the wall during a review meeting. Written records can also be made of what is important *to* and what is important *for* a pupil, distinguishing between the pupil's interests and priorities and those of their teachers and parents.

Parent partnerships

Accuracy in assessment is supported by the involvement of parents, who have important and unique information to contribute in building a picture of their child's learning and development. School practitioners need to work with a sense of partnership with parents, particularly in inclusive autism education, since they cannot expect to know and understand everything about the autistic pupil. Inviting parents to review meetings and consulting regularly with them are key processes within review, assessment and planning. Establishing equality within relationships is also important, where communication is open and there is a reciprocal exchange of information. Focusing on a pupil's competencies, what is working well in school and what the pupil particularly enjoys can also be critical to lessening parental anxiety and concern.

Pupil involvement

Observing pupils ensures that their views and perspectives are gathered as part of a continuous process of assessment and planning. Children express themselves strongly through their actions, and making observations of their behaviour is amongst the most powerful forms of listening to children, though it is also possible to ask them questions and listen to what they say. Some pupils are able to participate in more formal assessment processes and can be asked to review assessment information and attend formal meetings. Pupil participation in meetings is supported by the use of clear structures, visual information and visual schedules – for example, using a schedule to indicate what will be discussed first, second and third, and then removing these items as they are discussed. Case study 2 describes the involvement in the review and planning process of an autistic pupil who is experiencing anxiety in school.

Case study 2: Aiden

Staff have become increasingly concerned about Aiden, aged 10, who appears to have become more socially withdrawn and anxious in school. They have carried out observations in the classroom and at playtimes and have consulted with his parents, who report that he is increasingly reluctant to go to school. Aiden is spending more time by himself in school and is struggling in class in terms of his ability to focus on tasks and remember instructions. It is decided to hold a meeting to review Aiden's progress in school and plan appropriate support. Aiden's class teacher, the support worker who regularly works in his class, his parent and two outside agencies, the speech and language therapist and a specialist teacher, are invited to the meeting.

Though staff want to place Aiden's views about school at the heart of the review process, they believe that a meeting involving several adults will be too difficult for him. They arrange a pre-meeting between Aiden, his mother and the school SENCo, who was previously also Aiden's class teacher and knows him well. The SENCo outlines the structure of the meeting to Aiden by writing a list of things to discuss, including 'what I like about school', 'where I feel safe' and 'who helps me'. Items on this list are ticked off as each one is discussed, and the SENCo also has photographs of areas of the school for Aiden to reflect on. Aiden shares the fact that the garden is the only place he feels safe and that there is no one in school who helps him.

Following this, the review meeting discusses what is important to Aiden in school, using Aiden's comments and the information they have gathered from observation and their own reflections. It is felt that having time away from people is important to Aiden as well as having time to think about Minecraft, a computer game he feels passionately about and enjoys playing at home. The meeting also discusses what is not working in school at present and focuses on the fact that Aiden feels he has no one who helps him. Aiden's mother reports that, at home, Aiden constantly asks her if she loves him and that she is always giving him this reassurance, saying that she is happy to do so since she feels this is something he needs. The meeting discusses the fact that Aiden had experienced a particularly good relationship with a class teacher he had several years before, but has not formed any close relationships since that time. It is considered that what is important for Aiden at present is to experience the same emotional reassurances he gets at home in school and for there to be someone in school who Aiden feels cares for him and is thinking about him.

A plan of action is drawn up which identifies a key person for Aiden in school, the support worker who helps out in Aiden's class and who gets on well with him. It is felt that an important form of support for Aiden is for this key person to develop a closer relationship with him and provide verbal reassurances, telling Aiden regularly, 'You're okay' and 'It's okay' when he is attempting to do something. The plan of action also includes ensuring that Aiden experiences some non-social time each day in school. It is decided that he should have regular access to the garden, where he can have time away from people. It is also agreed that he should be allowed to have some time in school each day to think about his favourite computer game, and that there should not be the expectation by adults that he is always 'on task' and 'socially present'.

It is important to focus on pupils' competencies, strengths and interests when involving them in review processes. All of us feel less comfortable talking about things we find difficult, and this is the same for children, including children with autism. Children and young people may need help to express their views, and key aspects of support are set out here:

- offer choices or possibilities, preferably in visual form;
- give extra time for the pupil to respond;
- respect the pupil's opinions, interests and choices;
- avoid persuasion or prompting to support a predetermined outcome or idea;
- build self-confidence by *really* listening to the child or young person, trying to understand what they are saying and not jumping to conclusions.

From practitioner, parent and pupil discussions, an action plan is drawn up which identifies next steps in learning as well as important support strategies and learning opportunities. Assessment of the ways in which a pupil has developed is also an outcome of these discussions. For pupils with autism, assessment of progress in relation to curriculum areas, such as literacy and numeracy, using criteria designed for all learners will be a feature. However, what will also be crucially important is assessment of their development in other areas of learning, notably social-emotional development, linguistic and communicative development, and physical development. Social interaction, social communication and making sense of social experience are key areas of difficulty in autism and a strong focus for educational support. These areas of learning for the autistic pupil often require more focused teaching and learning than for the typically developing pupil. It is also the case that development in these areas often occurs atypically for people with autism, who may develop particular ways of communicating, being with others and participating in the social world. Slightly different outcomes in relation to these areas of learning operate for the autistic pupil and are set out ahead.

Learning outcomes in relation to atypical development

Learning outcomes in relation to social communication are organized here under the key competencies of participation, communication and thinking. Since stress caused by social demands and sensory processing difficulty is a prevalent feature of autism, a preliminary set of outcomes relating to emotional well-being is also included. These four areas of competency are presented separately for ease of use, but should be viewed as inextricably linked and parts of a developmental whole. In identifying patterns of behaviour, it is useful to refer to learning outcomes within one area of competency whilst maintaining an awareness that other dimensions of learning and development are also occurring. Children's ability to participate with others, for example, is interlinked with their competencies in communication, bodily co-ordination and self-regulation, but you may make the judgement that interacting with others, participating in social routines and enjoying the company of peers are a pupil's key areas of learning at this point in time and so focus on learning outcomes in relation to participation.

  In making assessments of progress, it is important to look for patterns of behaviour that occur over a period of time and that give rise to a sense of the pupil having moved forward in terms of what they understand and can do. Assessment of a pupil's progress in relation to learning outcomes must always be in consideration of the learning context. For all children, what they know and can do is linked to the context in which it occurs, and for pupils with autism this is particularly the case. Following frameworks for assessment that take a sociocultural approach, such as the early years curriculum Te Whāriki (New Zealand Ministry of Education, 1996), the learning outcomes are presented here alongside key questions about environmental features, influences and supports, and possible barriers to learning. Of key consideration will be the language context, the expectations of others, roles and relationships, the consistency of routines, and the quality of the physical and sensory environment. Questions about these and other important influences should always be taken into consideration when reflecting on learning outcomes, progress and future planning.

EMOTIONAL WELL-BEING

Learning outcomes The pupil should learn/have:	*Key contexts for reflection and possible barriers to learning*
A feeling of safety within the educational placement	What are the first and last routines of the day? Are these consistently carried out? Are ordinary routines and expectations communicated as visual information within the setting? How consistent are routines? Is the pupil adequately prepared for changes to routine and situations where ordinary expectations change? What arrangements are made for changes in staffing? How are transitions managed and is the pupil prepared beforehand?
Developing ability to comply with ordinary routines and expectations	
Developing capacity to tolerate managed change	How much control does the pupil have over what they are expected to do? Is the balance between choice and direction appropriate to the pupil's needs? Are rules, boundaries and hazards communicated clearly?
Developing capacity to tolerate unexpected events and/or uncertainty about events	How far is the pupil's non-compliance with routines, expectations and rules seen by adults as the possible result of stress related to features within the physical and/or social environment? Are adults able to identify early signs of stress in a pupil and take effective action? How do adults respond to spinning, stimming and rocking behaviours in a pupil? Do adults know that a pupil who is performing well academically may nevertheless be experiencing stress – for example, in relation to change, social expectations, fear of getting things wrong?
Increasing responsibility within whole-school and special events	
Ability to comply with rules that are clearly communicated	
Developing capacity to express views in relation to a range of choices	
Developing capacity to understand how to keep self and others safe from harm	What arrangements are made for personal belongings and need for personal space in the setting? Are these appropriate to pupil's needs? Where does the pupil feel most comfortable? Are opportunities provided for non-social time, quiet spaces and the pursuit of special interests?
Developing awareness of physical self	Do adults consider the impact of the sensory environment on the pupil? Are sensory audits carried out and reasonable environmental adjustments made to meet the pupil's sensory needs?
Ability to identify and name widening range of feelings	Is there a key adult in a social-emotional support role within the setting? How do they gain and share information about the pupil with practitioners, parents and peers?
Developing capacity to regulate feelings and self-calm in relation to social and/or sensory experience	How are pupils emotionally supported in relation to eating, washing and toileting? How are bodily functions visualized and explained? Do adults point out the physical signs that the pupil is hot, hurt, hungry, unwell or tired?
Developing capacity to tolerate fears about certain places or events	How do parents and staff collaborate over eating, toileting and daily living skills? How is independence promoted? Do adults enable pupils to express their views and take part in decision making? Does the pupil's individual learning plan address proprioception and gross motor development?

Does the environment contain visual information about emotions? Is a mirror available? Do adults point out other pupils' feelings by directing pupil's attention to their facial expressions? How do adults instruct pupils visually about the differences between similar feelings? How is emotion linked to experience within learning contexts?

How do adults manage situations that are fearful for the pupil? Is it possible to provide graduated experiences in relation to fears? How are parents supported in relation to their child's fears and levels of stress?

Examples of appropriate learning opportunities and supports

Information displayed visually – for example, for timetables, choices, rewards and routines.

Clear and consistent communication around routines and changes to routine – language appropriate to level of the pupil's understanding.

Regular non-social breaks.

Programme of gross and fine motor exercises – exercises embedded in ordinary routines and activities.

Reading picture books in relation to food, toileting and feelings. Desensitization techniques.

Support for self-regulation – for example, use of gentle interaction, music, materials for sensory feedback (e.g. weighted lap-pads).

Soothing sensory toys, relaxation activities, mindfulness techniques and low-arousal environments.

Emotion posters, photographs and freeze frames to identify facial expressions and link to real-life experiences.

Emotion scales which visually communicate differing intensities of feeling and encourage conscious modulation of feeling.

Good communication systems for practitioners and between home and school – for example, home-school books, texting, regular review meetings scheduled.

PARTICIPATION

Learning outcomes The pupil should learn/have:	*Key contexts for reflection and possible barriers to learning*
Enjoyment of own special interests and strengths	Is the pupil viewed as 'essentially different to' or 'essentially the same as' other pupils? Is this reflected in how special interests, strengths and ways of doing things are recognized, valued and accommodated? How do pupils describe themselves and each other?
Developing capacity to enjoy child-led one-to-one interactions with an adult	What patterns of activity in play and interaction exist in this setting? What are the sensory, communicative, physical and intellectual demands of each of these? How do individual pupils participate in ways that are different and the same? How much enjoyment do children derive from their play?
Enjoyment of relationships with pupils in a small structured group setting	
Experiences of appreciation by peers	
Developing capacity to participate in mutually enjoyable play and interaction routines with another pupil in ordinary everyday contexts	What cultural resources do children draw on in their play and interactions? How do adults investigate this? Do children have access to clear, visually based descriptions of their cultural routines? How often do adults make observations of children's play and interactions? Do adults value all children's preferences in play? How are play opportunities and the play space organized? How are play materials selected? What opportunities are there for visualizing aspects of children's play and games? What role do adults have when children are playing?
Experiences of participating with a wider circle of peers in ordinary contexts	
Developing capacity to show concern for other pupils	In what ways do adults provide support for group processes – for example, identifying suitable playmates, pairing children, providing resources to meet individual and shared interests? Do pupils have access to clear, visually based explanations for what to do and say in specific social situations?
Interest in following another pupil's ideas	What social roles are children adopting in play and interaction? Are these appropriate to the social context and themes of the play?
Experiences of shared cultural routines in play and interaction with a small number of peers in ordinary everyday contexts	What opportunities exist for explaining the language of more challenging social experiences – for example, winning and losing, being first, making mistakes, not being chosen? Are there opportunities for explaining the language involved in these experiences – that is, that 'winning and losing' does not mean the same as being 'good and bad'? Is waiting a turn provided as a concrete and visual experience?
Feelings of closeness, enjoyment and trust with a small number of peers	What do adults do when a pupil is negatively judged or excluded from the group? What do adults do when a pupil negatively judges others? How is conflict thought about and managed by adults? Are adults aware that pupils with autism are more likely to be teased and bullied by other pupils in school?
Developing appropriate strategies for dealing with conflict	
Developing capacity to participate in emotionally challenging social experience	Is there an appropriate balance between the provision of social experiences of participation and non-social breaks from participating? How do adults feel about a pupil who is on their own?

Examples of appropriate learning opportunities and supports

Systematic investigation into and sound understanding of children's cultural routines, play cultures and the nature of social relations within the setting.

Careful consideration of play materials and organization of the play space. Provision of toys that provide for a range of play interests, including sensory and physical play, with practitioners thinking creatively about what is a toy.

Structures provided for 'unstructured times' – for example, choose boards, alternative activities, alternative places to go.

Introduction of playground games that are 'autism-friendly' – that is, games that have a strong sensory, visual, or physical component, that have clear interactive turns and do not require a high level of verbal language.

Clear indications for the beginning and ending of activities and for transition between activities.

Friendship groups with a carefully selected group of peers who show an interest in each other or share common interests.

Pupils selected for ordinary activities on basis of friendship, rather than ability or because another pupil is a 'good role model'.

Social Stories ™ and social information posters.

Learning Stories and other visual descriptions of the sequence of events in an activity or game.

Individualized explanations of pupil participation, supported with mapping and other forms of visual information.

Visual behaviour charts that are colour-coded – for example, using green for 'Do' and red for 'Don't' behaviours.

Putting parents in touch with each other as a way of supporting friendship in and out of school.

COMMUNICATION

Learning outcomes The pupil should learn/have:	*Key contexts for reflection and possible barriers to learning*
Developing capacity for communicating needs, wants and interests with an adult	Are adults able to recognize pupils' communication in all its forms and even when it is delayed, weak or indirect? How aware are adults of their own communication, verbal and non-verbal, with pupils? In what ways do adults simplify their language and communication and support it with visual information, gesture and sign? Do they speak slowly and clearly, and without overusing a raised voice? Are questions supported by visual choices?
Developing capacity to notice and attend to other pupils' non-verbal and verbal communication	
Experiences of communication with peers in a supported group setting	What forms of communication are used in children's play and interactions? How do adults investigate and record this? Are all forms of pupils' communication equally valued – for example, looking with interest, hugs, shared use of space? How do pupils make sense of and engage with each other's communication? Do pupils' communication forms 'fit' their play and interaction routines?
Enjoyment of non-verbal communicative experiences with a peer in ordinary everyday contexts	
Increasing variation in non-verbal forms of communication used in ordinary contexts	In what circumstances is the pupil optimally attentive to other people's communication – for example, who, where, when, what? How does the pupil's communication relate to the emotion involved in a situation – for example, becomes muddled when upset?
Increasing confidence in and enjoyment of vocalizing within social contexts	In what ways do adults and pupils appreciate socially appropriate use of language in whatever form – for example, repeated questions, echolalia, borrowed sentences that are nevertheless appropriate to what is being communicated? Where and when is echolalia used? How do adults help pupils 'find the words'?
Developing capacity to contribute verbal communication in ordinary contexts	
Increasing effectiveness in communication in terms of the social responses of others	What is the balance between verbal and non-verbal communication within the general group and within smaller distinct peer groups? What is the flow and quality of pupils' talk and what do they talk about? How is media culture used?
Increasing flexibility in communication given who is being communicated with and what is being communicated about	What misunderstandings occur within communication and how are they resolved? Who notices difference in terms of communication and what do they do as a response? What is the basis of any conflict between pupils? Are adults/children providing sufficient time for responses in communication?
	Is there consistency of communication across adults and across home and school? How is information about the pupil's communication shared between adults? Are adults given opportunities to communicate their feelings and ideas about their work with pupils?

Examples of appropriate learning opportunities and supports

Systematic investigation into children's cultures of communication within the setting, taking in general features as well as the specific features of the individual pupil and their smaller peer group, if one exists.

Supported experiences of non-verbal communication in small-group situations, using activities that involve rhythm, back-and-forth experience and coordinated movement and that maximize children's enjoyment of each other's communication.

Supported experiences of verbal communication in small-group situations, using activities that use scripts, call and response and repetition and that 'play' with verbal language in communication.

Provision of a range of means for communication, including pictures, objects and ICT.

Role play.

Use of visual prompts for social communication in ordinary contexts – for example, visually prompt 'hand up to answer', 'good listening' poster.

Individualized explanations of children's communication, supported with visual information.

Explanations of social understandings and norms within the group and setting, together with ideas about what a pupil can say and do in specific contexts.

MAKING SENSE OF THE WORLD

Learning outcomes The pupil should learn/have:	*Key contexts for reflection and possible barriers to learning*
Opportunities to reflect on own experiences that are visually represented and organized	How are pupil's experiences visualized and mapped within ordinary classroom practice? Do adults model simple ways of thinking about experience – for example, first this happened, then this? Is there proper consideration of what is meaningful for an autistic person – that is, that emotion may be linked more to external appearance than inner intentions and thoughts?
Developing capacity to recognize ideas and concepts represented as photos, pictures, words, symbols and numbers	How are links made between representations of a single idea/concept – for example, is the written form of a number routinely accompanied with its visual representation, do pictures accompany words? Are pupils given sufficient time to talk about their special interests? How often is new learning based on pupils' interests and strengths?
Developing socially based strategies for making sense of the world – for example, watching others, making comments, asking questions	What do pupils talk about and how has this changed over time? In what ways are they encouraged and supported to watch others, comment, ask questions? Do adults routinely 'map' ideas in visual ways that demonstrate the links between one thing and another? Is 'choice' presented in clear and visual ways?
Increasing interest in making links between two or more items – for example, experiences, ideas, objects, routines	Do adults have good awareness of the cognitive demands of different question forms? How do adults deal with questions that involve abstract concepts – for example, religious concepts?
Developing capacity to enjoy stories and information not directly linked to own experience	When does the pupil's freedom of choice need to be restrained, expanded or controlled? How are stories chosen and are adults aware of narratives in terms of their visual and sensory content? How are pupils supported to generate and organize thought around a topic? Are they given access to collective ideas within the group – for example, through brainstorming activities? Is a range of methods for recording ideas available? Are alternative methods of recording used – for example, ones based in ICT?
Developing capacity for creating socially meaningful sequences of events	
Increasing awareness of and interest in the social world, including roles, relationships and responsibilities	How do adults react when pupils make 'mistakes'? Is a 'mistake' clearly differentiated from 'being bad'? Are 'thinking and talking about a topic' presented as a separate task to 'recording my ideas'? Are pupils given opportunities to map 'all my ideas', regardless of whether relevant to a topic, and then being supported to choose between these?
Increasing confidence in dramatic and role play	How do adults describe and explain social roles and relationships in school, at home and in the community? Are pupils provided with clear ideas about expectations in relation to these?
Increasing confidence to generate more than one idea in relation to a topic	How do adults talk about and describe 'thoughts'? In what ways do adults visualize mental processes – for example, thinking, remembering, deciding? How are pupils helped to exert control over their thoughts?

Examples of appropriate learning opportunities and supports

Visual methods for representing mental concepts – for example, visual representation of numbers 1 to 10, use of symbols and pictures to accompany words.

Visual methods for describing links between ideas – for example, mind maps in simple and more complex forms.

Visual methods for harnessing shared ideas – for example, Thinking Maps®.

Visual methods for explaining meanings of concepts – for example, word maps that include word meanings and associations, opposite and similar words, and that also focus on the look, sound and grammatical forms of a word.

Methods for visualizing and organizing the relation between thought, feeling and action – for example, the Incredible Five-Point Scale.

Clear and visual explanations of social rules and norms.

Use of colour-coding to highlight same and/or different ideas, experiences, rules and so forth.

Social maps for relationships and hierarchies within home, school and community.

Planners, flow-charts, calendars, sequences, maps, timers and so forth to support personal organization and the recording of ideas.

Adult knowledge about developmental levels of question forms – that is, naming, describing, instructing, sequencing and predicting.

Short forms of recording – for example, lists, labels, cloze procedure, sorting and sticking, and alternative forms of recording information – for example, scribing and dictating.

Identifying SMART targets

The process of target setting involves recognizing pupil achievement and planning for their next steps in learning. The target refers to the expected outcome of further learning support, with important features of the learning context forming an integral part of the target – that is, what the pupil should learn next *within* planned-for environmental conditions. Targets should be personal and relate to the child's actual lived experiences, interests and concerns, rather than to a more impersonal set of developmental norms. They should take account of what professionals and parents believe to be important for a pupil's learning, but also of what is important to the pupil, what they value, want and show an interest in.

Identifying targets that are SMART (i.e. specific, measurable, achievable, realistic and time-bound) supports good practice. However, given the highly integrated and complex nature of social communication, identifying SMART targets in relation to areas of learning and development is far from a straightforward task (Conn, 2014b). In defining SMART targets, it is vitally important to identify a learning outcome in relation to specific features of the pupil's environment – that is, to specific people, events, practices, routines or places. Figure 4.1 illustrates this process, showing how a general learning outcome about the pupil's participation in more challenging social experiences is made SMART by the specification of *which* experiences, as well as the proposed contexts for learning and nature of any support. Case study 3 provides more in the way of an illustration, outlining the process of SMART target setting for a pupil with autism who is experiencing difficulty with winning and losing when playing games with other children.

Case study 3: Ruby

Ruby, aged 8, finds that winning and losing are difficult social experiences in relation to playing board games with other children, and when she is carrying out competitive play at playtimes. At these times, she will become upset and angry when she does not win, insisting every time that she should be the winner. Staff identify an important area of learning is in relation to social participation and make reference to this framework for their observations and assessments. They identify a learning outcome for Ruby is the development of a greater capacity to participate appropriately in social experience that is emotionally challenging and discuss specific contexts for learning and possible learning supports. Through reflection on learning contexts and their own practice, staff realize that being 'good and bad' are reinforced as states that children must either always aspire to or must never be. They discuss how Ruby's understanding of 'winning' and 'losing' might be equated for her with these powerful concepts of 'good' and 'bad', and note that she also has problems with not being first in the line and with not being chosen to do something – for example, to be 'helper of the week'.

As a result of this reflection, staff identify a SMART target for Ruby that is based on specific events which regularly result in upset, and plan appropriate learning supports. They decide to focus on two weekly events, one where children are chosen to be 'helper of the week' and to have special responsibilities in class, and the other an assembly where children are given certificates for achievement in school. These are events where adult support for learning is easily accessible and are seen as starting points for Ruby's learning in this area of social participation. They set achievement criteria as a decrease in the number of upsets that occur as well as the length of time Ruby is upset and decide to record this information in a diary. Depending on the outcome of review of this target, staff identify future steps in learning as being able to participate more appropriately in competitive play and being supported to take turns at being first in the line at lining-up time.

SMART target	Learning supports	Achievement criteria
To be able to participate more appropriately in 'Student of the week' and certificate awards in assembly.	Individualised support for understanding of language and concepts that are related to winning and losing, eg. good/bad, first/last, win/lose, right/wrong, choose/reject. Possible use of word attribute maps to support understanding of ways in which these concepts are similar and ways in which they are different.	Incidence of upsets is reduced (specified amount). Duration of upsets is reduced (specified amount).
	Staff adjust language use so as not always to reinforce 'good' and 'bad'. Introduction of ideas such as 'a good loser and poor winner', and 'we learn from our mistakes'. Rehearse strategies with Ruby for self-calming, eg. encouraging her to reassure herself by saying 'It's OK', and teaching breathing techniques. Adults have greater tolerance of Ruby being upset on these occasions.	

PARTICIPATION

Learning outcomes	SMART target	Key contexts for reflection and possible barriers to learning
The child should learn/have:		

Developing capacity to participate in emotionally challenging social experience

General learning outcome is made 'SMART' by relating it to *specific* people, interactions and events – target includes adjustments of the environment, by adults etc.

What opportunities exist for explaining the language of more challenging social experiences – e.g., winning and losing, being first, making mistakes, not being chosen? Are there opportunities for explaining the language involved in these experiences – i.e., that 'winning and losing' does not mean the same as being 'good and bad'? Is waiting a turn provided as a concrete and visual experience?

Is there an appropriate balance between the provision of social experiences of participation and non-social breaks from participating? How do adults feel about a child who is on their own? How do adults feel about a child who is distressed?

Learning opportunities and supports

- Systematic investigation into and sound understanding of child   tural routines, play cultures and the nature of social relations within the setting.
- Careful consideration of play materials and organisation of the pl   . Provision of toys that provide for a range of play interests, including sensory and physical play, with p   ers thinking creatively about what is a toy.
- Introduction of playground games that are 'autism-friendly' – i.e.,   have a strong sensory, visual, physical component, that have clear interactive turns and do not require a   of verbal language.
- Clear indications for the beginning and ending of activities and fo   on between activities.
- Friendship groups with a carefully selected group of peers who s   terest in each other or share common interests.
- Children selected for ordinary activities on basis of friendship, r   ability or because another child is a 'good role model'.
- Social Stories™ and social information posters.
- Learning stories and other visual explanations of the sequen   in an activity or game.

- Individualized explanations of children's participation, supported with mapping and other forms of visual information.

- Visual behaviour charts that are colour-coded – e.g., using green for 'Do' and red for 'Don't' behaviours.
- Putting parents in touch with each other as way of supporting friendship in and out of school.

Figure 4.1 Process of SMART target setting in relation to specific learning contexts

It has already been noted that children's and young people's learning and development have an unknowable, underground quality and sometimes happen in unexpected ways. Teachers plan for next steps in learning, but sometimes these occur in relation to opportunities that have not been planned for. Plans need to be flexible therefore and maintain a focus on pupils' changing needs and interests. Nevertheless, it is important to think about ways to support pupil learning and frame what it is you are hoping to achieve in relation to this. Thinking about what it is that you are trying to do and identifying areas of learning help clarify for professionals the purpose of learning supports, particularly within the challenging area of support for social-emotional learning. Box 4.1 provides some examples of how to frame contextualized learning targets in relation to social communication.

Box 4.1   Examples of contextualized learning targets

Holly is able to . . . when / where . . .

James demonstrates an understanding of . . . when . . .

Ethan has opportunities to / access to . . . during . . .

Mason demonstrates appropriate strategies for . . . during . . .

Charlotte experiences appropriate adult response when / in relation to . . .

Mohammed experiences clear instruction for . . .

Zoe benefits from adults awareness / provision of . . . when . . .

Hailey is encouraged / helped to . . . through use of . . . when / during . . .

Elijah appropriately / flexibly communicates . . . when / in relation to . . .

Logan demonstrates an enjoyment of . . . when / with / by . . .

Megan shows increasing confidence to . . . when / with . . .

Demonstrating progress: Using the pupil as their own baseline

The atypical development that occurs for pupils with autism means that measurement of progress against standardized norms is of limited value. The often personalized nature of an autistic pupil's learning experiences makes local measures much more useful within inclusive education. The autism population is a highly diverse one, and it is often better to use the child themselves as the baseline measure for any progress. Figures 4.2a and 4.2b show observational mapping records of a pupil, Harry, aged 4, at two different time periods. Harry's use of the classroom space and range of interests were mapped several weeks after he joined the class as a baseline measure. At the end of a successful academic year for Harry, his

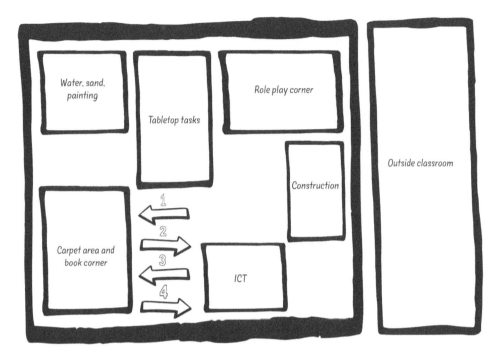

Figure 4.2a Mapping showing a pupil's restricted interests and use of space

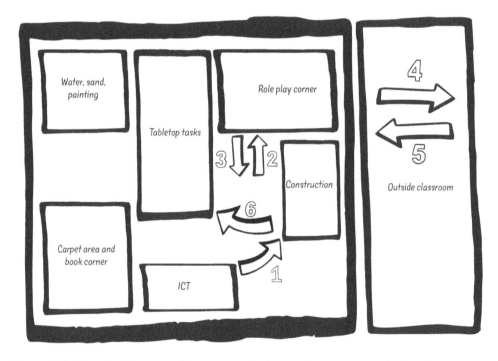

Figure 4.2b Mapping demonstrating progress in the pupil's engagement in the classroom

use of the classroom space was mapped again and demonstrated a much wider use of the space and engagement with a greater number of activities. This evidence, together with narrative descriptions of Harry's level of functioning from participant observations and parent accounts, contributed to the creation of a 'picture of development' that reflected Harry's good progress that year.

Learning progress can be measured in terms of the incidence of a behaviour that has been identified as significant, as well as its duration, frequency or cessation. Again, it is possible to use the pupil as their own baseline, measuring a behaviour over two or more time periods to see if a change has occurred. Behaviours that are deemed to be significant should have relevance to the child's or young person's actual level of functioning and experience, and should not be imposed as behaviours you believe they ought to be displaying. Equally, information about attainment should generally not be recorded within tick boxes because this gives insufficiently detailed information about the learning processes in which the pupil is participating, particularly processes of social-emotional learning that are rich and complex in nature. It is preferable to use descriptive information about specific interactions and events, since these are more valuable and have greater accuracy.

Finally, in demonstrating pupil progress, it is helpful to identify starting points in learning. Identifying a starting point, particularly in relation to social-emotional learning, is often a challenge for practitioners, but certain points in time are useful to consider. These include:

- when the pupil transfers to a new setting or begins a new class – for example, at the beginning of the academic year;
- when a new learning target has been identified and appropriate support strategies are in place;
- when a new learning context is introduced – for example, more focused work within a small group or use of a specific learning intervention.

Chapter 5

Compiling pupil profiles and evaluating practice

<table>
<tr><td>

Focus of this chapter:

- compiling profiles of pupils' attainments using methods that are particularly suited to autistic pupils
- important areas of practice to evaluate in inclusive autism education.

</td></tr>
</table>

Part of the process of assessment is to keep records of pupils' learning alongside evaluations of your own practice, including the effectiveness of support strategies, communication systems and environmental adjustments that are in place.

Profiling pupil attainment

Profiling pupil learning is about creating snapshots of significant moments in learning that capture what children and young people know and can do, and in what ways they are developing. Profiling should be a manageable task for practitioners and should not involve excessive amounts of information to record or read through. It is important to include detailed information, especially in relation to the social and cultural processes within a setting with which a pupil is learning to engage. What is profiled are the critical moments in learning when the child is taking a new interest in something, participating effectively in some way, persisting with something that challenges them or expressing an idea (Carr, 2001). Short forms of recording may be used, such as the annotation of photographs, brief summaries and single examples of a particular behaviour that has wider developmental significance.

Profiling should have a purpose, which could be one or more of the following:

- sharing attainment with the pupil or with parents;
- sharing information about the pupil's learning with other practitioners – for example, to ensure consistency of support and communication – or when a pupil transitions to a new group or setting;
- as evidence of attainment for pupil records.

A profile should reflect the personal learning experiences of the pupil and should be adapted to that. It should not be made to fit a standard pro forma, with the danger that important areas of learning activity are overlooked. Learning records used in early years education, which record children's learning in both visual and narrative format, are especially useful. It could be argued that inclusive autism education is most aligned with early years practice, which has a strong focus on young children's social-emotional learning and experiences of interactions and relationships. Early years practice often takes an observation-based approach to pedagogy, looking at the whole child within ordinary contexts and centrally using teacher reflection to understand the child's ways of making meaning and know how to support their learning and development. Early years learning records are typically a snapshot of development that can be shared with pupils, parents and practitioners. These records combine pictorial evidence of a critical moment in learning, in the form of a photograph or sequence of photographs or brief video footage, with a short descriptive passage about what the pupil is learning to do and why this is developmentally significant. What the pupil might learn next can also be recorded as next steps in learning. If learning records are shared with parents, they may also comment on related learning they have observed at home.

One-page profiles

One-page profiles are used in schools to provide concise, relevant and rich information about the quality of a pupil's learning experiences. They can be used with pupils of any age to record key pieces of information about what is important to a child or young person, in what ways they can best be supported, what are their strengths and how they help themselves. Crucially, one-page profiles include the pupil's point of view as a way of enabling practitioners to know and understand them in a more meaningful way. Sanderson et al. (2010) have produced a series of one-page profiles that record in different ways the views of the pupil and the views of others in relation to interests, needs and effective forms of support. The actual process of creating a profile is an important one since it supports the development of practitioner understanding and knowledge of the pupil within the context of the classroom and the school. Profiles should be updated every so often and develop as the pupil develops. They should also be current in the sense that they are linked to present-day curriculum topics and activities.

One-page profiles are provided here for Lucas, aged 11, and Isla, aged 6, both of whom are autistic. Though these two children have very different capacities in communication and interaction, it is possible to see how their profiles include similar areas of information about interests, strengths, ways of communicating and learning support needs. These are key areas for autistic pupils and will probably always form part of a one-page profile.

Lucas

What is important to me

My special interest is Doctor Who and I like to think about him a lot. I know lots of Doctor Who–related information.

Please give me some time each day to think about Doctor Who – it helps me to concentrate in class!!

I really like drawing pictures about Doctor Who too and am writing a book about him at the moment.

I love computer games, and I really enjoy playing action-adventure games with my friends at playtime.

My friends

Jacob

Harley

Mason – though we do fall out because we both want to be leaders when we play

Charlie – she's a girl and we know each other outside school too.

You can help me communicate if you:

- Give me time to 'switch off' my thoughts before I start listening to you
- Let me talk about my special interests sometimes – and just listen
- Explain what people mean when they do or say something I don't understand or find annoying
- Explain the meanings of little words and funny sayings – I don't usually have a problem with big words
- Know when I am feeling a bit stressed and give me some quiet time

I help myself by:

Walking away from situations and going to the quiet area.

Doing my 4-7-8 breathing exercises.

Having regular 'Me time' when I can think about my special interests.

I work best:

IN GROUP WORK when I am given one clear role – for example, group leader, listener or scribe.

IN WRITING TASKS when I know how much time I have got to complete the task – timers work well for me! And sometimes a support worker scribes for me.

When I know the teacher – otherwise I might be a bit unsettled.

Things you should know about me are:

I love sparkly things

I love playing with bubbles

I love dressing up like a princess

I love playing with people's hair, especially Miss Evan's

I love twirling

I like to spend some time each day by myself

I like watching other children playing from the top of the slide

I like listening to music – I find it very calming

Sometimes when I'm smiling I'm actually feeling really anxious

I don't like the smell of bananas – it makes me feel sick

I get very tired in the afternoons

❂✳✤✿❂

My friends are:

Miss Evans – we spend lots of time together

Elijah

❂✳✤✿❂

ISLA

You can communicate with me if you:

- Use only two or three words at a time
- Use my name first so that you get my attention before you start speaking
- Talk in a quiet, slow and calm voice
- Always show me as well as tell me (e.g. using objects, pictures and gestures)
- Use a prompt card instead of talking to me when I am stressed
- Use visual instruction posters to tell me the rules

PLEASE DON'T TALK TO ME WHEN I'M UPSET OR TIRED

WAIT UNTIL LATER IF YOU CAN

You can help me by:

Using my visual timetable to show me what is happening now and what is happening next.

Using my choose board to give me choices – but please remember to change the choices every so often because sometimes I get bored!

Telling me when a change is coming up – and giving me lots of reassurance when that happens. You can say, 'Isla, you're OK' in a soft voice.

Doing my OT exercises with me three times a week so that I get stronger.

Giving me some 'non-social' time and remembering not to talk to me then.

Creating a 'picture of development'

Part of the purpose of compiling pupil profiles is to create a 'picture of development' over time. This is especially important in relation to children's social-emotional learning and social communication, which are areas of learning and development that are hard to record except as descriptive accounts made over time. Compiling a series of profiles provides a narrative for the children's learning journey within a particular setting and will serve as evidence of starting points and attainment over more than one academic year. For children and young people with autism, it is helpful to organize profiles into the relevant areas of:

- personal, social and emotional development;
- communicative development;
- physical development;
- development in thinking and doing.

 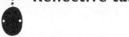 **Reflective task**

Tell other members of a discussion group what you are most proud of innovating in your setting for children with special educational needs and disability, particularly for those who are autistic.

Discuss what you would like to see in terms of development in relation to:

- the physical environment of the school
- your own understanding and knowledge
- the inclusiveness of the peer groups with which you work
- the whole-school community
- links with the wider community.

Evaluating practice

Evaluating practice in relation to pupils with special educational needs and disability requires consideration of the different influences on learning that exist for a pupil in a school setting. Children's learning and development are contingent upon direct influences, such as their experience of relationships with teachers and support staff and the learning supports they provide, but also upon processes that indirectly affect them. Factors such as school organization and management, the effectiveness of school communication systems, and cultural, attitudinal and value systems that exist within the whole-school setting and wider community are highly significant influences that must be taken into account. Research into effective practice in autism education suggests that pupil attainment is as affected by indirect influences as it is for all learners (AET, 2011). Schools operate as complex systems, where features in one part of the system impact on and bring about change in other parts of the system. Management expectations of staff, for example, may impact positively or negatively on individual practitioner belief in their competency, knowledge and capacity to meet the needs of the individual pupil, which in turn will determine degrees of success in doing this. These are hugely important considerations within inclusive education for children and young people with autism, and generally for pupils with special educational needs and disability, and make up important areas of reflection in evaluating practice. Table 5.1 sets out questions about important influences on pupil attainment and includes questions about the individual pupil's immediate learning experiences, but also questions about whole-school culture and practices, adult knowledge and understanding, peer group influences and features of the physical environment.

Evaluating communication systems in your setting

In evaluating practice in relation to inclusive autism education, a useful approach is to consider how well communication systems are operating in your setting. For children with autism, as for anyone who experiences communication difficulty, the effectiveness of communication in their school setting is critically important to their experience of teaching and learning. Communication must be considered at every level, not only adult-child communication but also the effectiveness of communication amongst all adults and children. Consider the effectiveness of communication:

- amongst practitioners;
- between practitioners and groups of children;
- amongst children;
- between practitioners and parents;
- within the network of support agencies.

Box 5.1 provides ideas for areas of evaluation in relation to the different communication systems that exist in your setting. Questions can be asked about which of these are operating, which are working well and which are a focus for further development.

Table 5.1 Evaluation of practice within different contexts

Context	Comment
Whole-school community Are all pupils viewed as capable of learning? Are there high expectations of all pupils? Is maximum inclusion an aspiration for all pupils with special educational needs and disability? Do senior managers have high expectations of staff? Is clear and open communication part of the culture of the school? What autism-related links are there with the local community?	
Adult understanding and knowledge Are adults supported in developing their knowledge and understanding of the autism spectrum? Is time allocated for observation, liaison and teacher reflection, review meetings and knowledge sharing? Are adults able to identify pupil strengths as well as needs? Is a range of communication systems available for: • practitioner conversations • listening to pupils • conversations with parents? Do adults view strong relationships with pupils as the starting pointing for learning?	
Peer group Are all pupils' interests, values and cultural activities seen as of interest and possible value? Are the similarities as well as differences between pupils noted? Are social interaction, play and friendship viewed as taking diverse forms for different pupils? Are pupils allowed to be by themselves? How are pupils supported in understanding and coping with challenging social situations?	
Individual pupil Is communication always appropriate to the pupil's level of understanding? Is visual information regularly made available – for example, as timetables, calendars, choices, charts, or visual instructions? Is there clear and consistent information around changes to routine? Is there a balance between support for academic learning and support for social, emotional and communicative development? Is time for special interests and non-social breaks regularly provided?	
The physical environment Is the physical environment clearly organized? How are pupils supported to know their environment? Are they consulted on environmental changes and adaptations? Do practitioners understand the sensory demands of the environment? Is there access to quiet areas, which have reduced sound as well as 'visual noise'?	

Box 5.1   Effective communication systems in inclusive autism education

Practitioners communicating:
Daily conversations
Liaison time
Observations of practice
Planning meetings
Target-setting meetings
Regular review meetings
Departmental meetings
Meetings with outside advisory agencies
Pupil profiles
Notice boards
Display boards
Training sessions and staff meetings
School blog or round-robin network

Parents communicating:
Home-school books
Early morning/end of
    day practitioner-parent
    conversations
Regular updates via phone, text,
    email
Regular review meetings
Half-termly/termly meetings
Snapshot learning logs
Pupil profiles
Photographs and video footage
Annotated work samples

Pupils communicating:
Verbal communication using simplified language and/or supported with
    visual information
Non-verbal communication for example, through actions, sounds,
    movement, distance, orientation
Structured group discussions and support for listening to others
Visual timetables, work schedules and calendars
Information posters

Maps
Visual information to help clarify instructions and explanations – for
    example, photographs, symbols, objects, signs, drawing
Visual representation of abstract concepts – for example, for number, time,
    relationships, waiting, turn taking
Written forms of communication
Online communication

References

American Psychiatric Association (APA) (2013) *Diagnostic and Statistical Manual of Mental Disorders*, 5th edn, Washington, DC: American Psychiatric Publishing Inc.

Autism Education Trust (AET) (2011) *What Is Good Practice in Autism Education?*, London: National Autistic Society/Centre for Research in Autism and Education.

Baron-Cohen, S., Scott, F. J., Allison, C., Williams, J., Bolton, P., Matthews, F. E. and Brayne, C. (2009) 'Prevalence of autism-spectrum conditions: UK school-based population study', *British Journal of Psychiatry*, 194: 500–9.

Bauminger, N. and Kasari, C. (2000) 'Loneliness and friendship in high-functioning children with autism', *Child Development*, 71: 447–56.

Bauminger, N. and Shulman, C. (2003) 'The development and maintenance of friendship in high-functioning children with autism', *Autism*, 7: 81–97.

Bauminger, N., Solomon, M., Aviezer, A., Heung, K., Brown, J. and Rogers, S. (2008) 'Friendship in high-functioning children with autism spectrum disorder: mixed and non-mixed dyads', *Journal of Autism and Developmental Disorders*, 38: 1211–29.

Bellanca, N., Biggeri, M. and Marchetta, F. (2011) 'An extension of the capability approach: towards a theory of dis-capability', *European Journal of Disability Research*, 5: 158–76.

Beresford, B. (1997) *Personal Accounts: Involving Disabled Children in Research*, London: The Stationery Office/Social Policy Research Unit.

Beresford, B., Tozer, R., Rabiee, P. and Sloper, P. (2004) 'Developing an approach to involving children with autistic spectrum disorders in a social care research project', *British Journal of Learning Disabilities*, 32, 180–85.

Beresford, B., Tozer, R., Rabiee, P. and Sloper, P. (2007) 'Desired outcomes for children and adolescents with autistic spectrum disorders', *Children and Society*, 21: 4–16.

Billington, T. (2006) 'Working with autistic children and young people: sense, experience and the challenges for services, policies and practices', *Disability and Society*, 21: 1–13.

Black, P. and Wiliam, D. (2003) ' "In praise of educational research": formative assessment', *British Educational Research Journal*, 29: 623–37.

Bogdashina, O. (2003) *Sensory Perceptual Issues in Autism and Asperger Syndrome*, London and Philadelphia: Jessica Kingsley Publishers.

Bronfenbrenner, U. (1979) *The Ecology of Human Development*, Cambridge, MA: Harvard University Press.

Burke, J. (2012) ' "Some kids climb up; some kids climb down": culturally constructed play-worlds of children with impairments', *Disability and Society*, 27: 965–81.

Buron, K. D. and Curtis, M. (2012) *The Incredible 5-Point Scale: Assisting Students in Understanding Social Interactions and Controlling Their Emotional Responses*, Shawnee Mission, KS: Autism Asperger Publishing Co.

Carr, M. (2001) *Assessment in Early Childhood Settings: Learning Stories*, Los Angeles, London, New Delhi, Singapore and Washington, DC: SAGE.

Centers for Disease Control (CDC) (2015) *Data and Statistics: Autism Spectrum Disorders: Prevalence*. Online: http://www.cdc.gov/ncbddd/autism/data.html (accessed 13 June 2015).

Cesaroni, L. and Garber, M. (1991) 'Exploring the experience of autism through firsthand accounts', *Journal of Autism and Developmental Disorders*, 21: 303–13.

Chamberlain, B., Kasari, C. and Rotheram-Fuller, E. (2007) 'Involvement or isolation? The social networks of children with autism in regular classrooms', *Journal of Autism and Developmental Disorders*, 37: 230–42.

Christensen, P. and James, A. (2008) 'Childhood diversity and commonality: some methodological insights', in P. Christensen and A. James (eds.) *Research with Children: Perspectives and Practices*, New York and London: Routledge, 156–72.

Clark, A. (2005) 'Ways of seeing: using the Mosaic approach to listen to young children's perspectives', in A. Clark, A. T. Kjørholt and P. Moss (eds.) *Beyond Listening: Children's Perspectives on Early Childhood Services*, Bristol: Policy Press, 29–49.

Clark, A. and Moss, P. (2005) *Spaces to Play: More Listening to Young Children Using the Mosaic Approach*, London: National Children's Bureau.

Clark, A. and Moss, P. (2011) *Listening to Young Children: The Mosaic Approach*, 2nd edn, London: National Children's Bureau.

Conn, C. (2007) *Using Drama with Children on the Autism Spectrum*, Brackley, UK: Speechmark.

Conn, C. (2014a) *Autism and the Social World of Childhood: A Sociocultural Perspective on Theory and Practice*, Abingdon, Oxon and New York: Routledge.

Conn, C. (2014b) 'Investigating the social engagement of children with autism in mainstream schools for the purpose of identifying learning targets', *Journal of Research in Special Educational Needs*, 14: 153–59.

Corsaro, W. A. and Johannesen, B. O. (2007) 'The creation of new cultures in peer interaction', in J. Valsiner and A. Rosa (eds.) *The Cambridge Handbook of Sociocultural Psychology*, New York: Cambridge University Press, 444–59.

Davidson, J. and Henderson, V. L. (2010) ' "Travel in parallel with us for a while": sensory geographies in autism', *The Canadian Geographer*, 54: 462–75.

Department for Children, Schools and Families (DCSF) (2008a) *The Early Years Foundation Stage. Effective Practice: Observation, Assessment and Planning*. Online: www.ndna.org.uk/Resources/NDNA/Generic%20Folders%202/10/33.%20EYFS%20Observation_%20assessing%20and%20planning.pdf (accessed 16 November 2013).

Department for Children, Schools and Families (DCSF) (2008b) *Personalised Learning: A Practical Guide*. Online: http://webarchive.nationalarchives.gov.uk/20130401151715/https://www.education.gov.uk/publications/eOrderingDownload/00844–2008DOMEN.pdf (accessed 20 January 2014).

Department for Education (DfE) (2014) *Statistical First Release. Special Educational Needs in England: January 2014.* Online: https://www.gov.uk/government/organisa tions/department-for-education (accessed 7 November 2015).

Department for Education/Department of Health (DfE/DoH) (2015) *Special Educational Needs and Disability Code of Practice: 0 to 25 years.* Online: https://www.gov.uk/gov ernment/uploads/system/uploads/attachment_data/file/398815/SEND_Code_of_Prac tice_January_2015.pdf (accessed 13 June 2015).

Dickins, M. (2008) *Listening to Young Disabled Children*, London: National Children's Bureau.

Elwood, J. and Murphy, P. (2015) 'Editorial: assessment systems as cultural scripts: a soci-ocultural theoretical lens on assessment practice and products', *Assessment in Educa-tion: Principles, Policy and Practice*, 22: 182–92.

Emam, M. M. and Farrell, P. (2009) 'Tensions experienced by teachers and their views of support for pupils with autism spectrums disorders in mainstream schools', *European Journal of Special Needs Education*, 24: 407–22.

European Agency for Development in Special Needs Education (EADSNE) (2009) *Assess-ment for Learning and Pupils with Special Educational Needs.* Online: http://www. european-agency.org/sites/default/files/assessment-for-Learning-full-paper.pdf (accessed 18 January 2014).

Fawcett, M. (2009) *Learning through Child Observation*, 2nd edn, London and Philadel-phia: Jessica Kingsley.

Florian, L. (2008) 'Inclusion: special or inclusive education: future trends', *British Journal of Special Education*, 35: 202–8.

Frederickson, N. and Cline, T. (2009) *Special Educational Needs, Inclusion and Diversity*, 2nd edn, Berkshire, UK: Open University Press.

Frith, U. and Happé, F. (1999) 'Theory of mind and self-consciousness: what is it like to be autistic?', *Mind and Language*, 14: 1–22.

Gerland, G. (1997) *A Real Person: Life on the Outside*, London: Souvenir Press.

Grandin, T. (2006) *Thinking in Pictures and Other Reports from My Life with Autism*, 2nd edn, London, Berlin, New York and Sydney: Bloomsbury.

Gray, C. (1994) *Comic Strip Conversations: Illustrated Interactions That Teach Conversation Skills to Students with Autism and Related Disorders*, Arlington, VA: Future Horizons.

Harrington, C., Foster, M., Rodger, S. and Ashburner, J. (2013) 'Engaging young people with autism spectrum disorder in research interviews', *British Journal of Learning Dis-abilities*, 42: 153–61.

Humphrey, N. and Lewis, S. (2008) ' "Make me normal": the views and experiences of pupils on the autistic spectrum in mainstream secondary schools', *Autism*, 12: 23–46.

Hyerle, D. N. and Alper, L. S. (2011) *Student Successes with Thinking Maps®: School-Based Research, Results, and Models for Achievement Using Visual Tools*, 2nd edn, Thousand Oaks: Corwin.

James, A. (1999) 'Learning to be friends: participant observation amongst English school-children (The Midlands, England)', in C. W. Watson (ed.) *Being There: Fieldwork in Anthropology*, London and Sterling, VA: Pluto Press, 98–120.

James, A., Jenks, C. and Prout, A. (1998) *Theorizing Childhood*, Cambridge, MA: Polity Press.

Jarrold, C. and Conn, C. (2011) 'The development of pretend play in autism', in A. Pellegrini (ed.) *Oxford Handbook of the Development of Play*, New York and London: Oxford University Press, 308–21.

Jones, G., English, A., Guldberg, K., Jordan, R., Richardson, P. and Waltz, M. (2009) *Educational Provision for Children and Young People on the Autism Spectrum Living in England: Review of Current Practice, Issues and Challenges*, London: Autism Education Trust.

Jordan, R. (2005) 'Autistic spectrum disorders', in A. Lewis and B. Norwich (eds.) *Special Teaching for Special Children? Pedagogies for Inclusion*, Maidenhead: Open University Press, 110–22.

Jordan, R. and Powell, S. (1995) *Understanding and Teaching Children with Autism*, Chichester: Wiley.

Kasari, C., Chamberlain, B. and Bauminger, N. (2001) 'Social emotions and social relationships in autism: can children with autism compensate?', in J. Burack, T. Charman, N. Yirimiya and P. Zelazo (eds.) *The Development of Autism: Perspectives from Theory and Research*, Mahwah, NJ: Lawrence Erlbaum, 281–94.

Kasari, C. and Smith, T. (2013) 'Interventions in schools for children with autism spectrum disorder: methods and recommendations', *Autism*, 17: 254–67.

Lecavalier, L., Leone, S. and Wiltz, J. (2006) 'The impact of behaviour problems on caregiver stress in young people with autism spectrum disorders', *Journal of Intellectual Disability Research*, 50: 172–83.

Mesibov, G., Shea, V. and Schopler, E. (2004) *The TEACCH Approach to Autism Spectrum Disorders*, New York: Springer.

Milton, D. (2012) 'On the ontological status of autism: the 'Double Empathy Problem', *Disability and Society*, 27: 883–87.

New Zealand Ministry of Education (1996) *Te Whāriki: Early Childhood Curriculum*, Wellington: Learning Media. Online: http://www.educate.ece.govt.nz/~/media/Educate/Files/Reference%20Downloads/whariki.pdf (accessed 10 January 2010).

Newschaffer, C. J., Croen, L. A., Daniels, J., Giarelli, E., Grether, J. K., Levy, S. E., Mandell, D. S., Miller, L. A., Pinto-Martin, J., Reaven, J., Reynolds, A. M., Rice, C. E., Schendel, D. and Windham, G. C. (2007) 'The epidemiology of autism spectrum disorders', *Annual Review of Public Health*, 28: 235–58.

Nichols, S., Moravcik, G. M. and Tetenbaum, S. P. (2009) *Girls Growing Up on the Autism Spectrum: What Parents and Professionals Should Know about the Pre-teen and Teenage Years*, London: Jessica Kingsley Publishers.

Ochs, E., Kremer-Sadlik, T., Sirota, K. G. and Solomon, O. (2004) 'Autism and the social world: an anthropological perspective', *Discourse Studies*, 6: 147–83.

Ochs, E., Kremer-Sadlik, T., Solomon, O. and Sirota, K. G. (2001) 'Inclusion as social practice: views of children with autism', *Social Development*, 10: 399–419.

Powell, S. and Jordan, R. (1993) 'Diagnosis, intuition and autism', *British Journal of Special Education*, 20: 26–29.

Preece, D. and Jordan, R. (2009) 'Obtaining the views of children and young people with autism spectrum disorders about their experience of daily life and social care support', *British Journal of Learning Disabilities*, 38: 10–20.

Sanderson, H. and Lewis, J. (2012) *A Practical Guide to Delivering Personalisation: Person-Centred Practice in Health and Social Care*, London and Philadelphia: Jessica Kingsley Publishers.

Sanderson, H., Smith, T. and Wilson, L. (2010) *One-Page Profiles in Schools: A Guide*, Cheshire: HSA Press.

Schopler, E. (1994) 'Behavioural priorities for autism and related developmental disorders', in E. Schopler and G. B. Mesibov (eds.) *Behavioural Issues in Autism*, New York: Plenum Press, 55–80.

Sen, A. (1992) *Inequality Reexamined*, Cambridge, MA: Harvard University Press.

Shephard, C. and Treseder, P. (2002) *Participation: Spice It Up! Practical Tools for Engaging Children and Young People in Planning and Consultations*, Cardiff: Save the Children Fund.

Sinclair, J. 2009. *Why I Dislike "Person First" Language*. Online: http://autismmythbusters.com/general-public/autistic-vs-people-with-autism/jim-sinclair-why-i-dislike-person-first-language/ (accessed 17 August 2015).

Straus, J. N. (2013) 'Autism as culture', in L. J. Davis (ed.) *The Disability Studies Reader*, 4th edn, New York and Abingdon, UK: Routledge, 460–84.

Terzi, L. (2005) 'Beyond the dilemma of difference: the capability approach to disability and special educational needs', *Journal of Philosophy of Education*, 39: 443–59.

Thomas, C. (2013) 'Disability and impairment', in J. Swain, S. French, C. Barnes and C. Thomas (eds.) *Disabling Barriers-enabling Environments*, 3rd edn, London, Thousand Oaks, New Delhi and Singapore: SAGE, 9–16.

Tudge, J. and Hogan, D. (2005) 'An ecological approach to observations of children's everyday lives', in S. Greene and D. Hogan (eds.) *Researching Children's Experience: Methods and Approaches*, London, Thousand Oaks and New Delhi: SAGE, 102–22.

UN General Assembly (1989) *Convention on the Rights of the Child*, Document A/RES/44/25 (12 December), New York: United Nations.

Veale, A. (2005) 'Creative methodologies in participatory research with children', in S. Greene and D. Hogan (eds.) *Researching Children's Experience: Methods and Approaches*, London, Thousand Oaks and New Delhi: SAGE, 253–72.

Watson, N. (2012) 'Theorising the lives of disabled children: how can disability theory help?', *Children and Society*, 26: 192–202.

Webster, A., Feiler, A., Webster, V. and Lovell, C. (2004) 'Parental perspectives on early intensive intervention for children diagnosed with autistic spectrum disorder', *Early Childhood Research*, 2: 25–49.

Welsh Government (2014) *Legislative Proposals for Additional Learning Needs. White Paper*. Online: http://gov.wales/docs/dcells/publications/140522-consultation-document-en.pdf. (accessed 7 November 2015).

Wenger, E. (2009) 'A social theory of learning', in K. Illeris (ed.) *Contemporary Theories of Learning*, London and New York: Routledge, 209–18.

Westcott, H. L. and Littleton, K. S. (2005) 'Exploring meaning in interviews with children', in S. Greene and D. Hogan (eds.) *Researching Children's Experience: Methods and Approaches*, London, Thousand Oaks and New Delhi: SAGE, 141–57.

Wickenden, M. (2010) *Teenage Worlds, Different Voices: An Ethnographic Study of Identity and the Lifeworlds of Disabled Teenagers Who Use Augmentative and Alternative Communication*, unpublished PhD thesis, University of Sheffield.

Wiliam, D. and Leahy, S. (2007) 'A theoretical foundation for formative assessment', in J. H. McMillan (ed.) *Formative Classroom Assessment: Theory into Practice*, New York: Teachers College Press, 29–42.

Wilkinson, K. and Twist, L. (2010) *Autism and Educational Assessment: UK Policy and Practice*. Slough, UK: National Foundation for Educational Research.

Williams, D. (1996) *Autism: An Inside-Out Approach*, London and Philadelphia: Jessica Kingsley Publisher.

Woodhead, M. and Faulkner, D. (2008) 'Subjects, objects or participants? Dilemmas of psychological research with children', in P. Christensen and A. James (eds.) *Research with Children: Perspectives and Practices*, 2nd edn, New York and London: Routledge, 10–39.

Index